THE IMITATION OF CHRIST

A Modern Reading

THE IMITATION OF CHRIST

Thomas à Kempis

A Modern Reading by
Bernard Bangley

HIGHLAND BOOKS

Copyright © 1983 Bernard Langley

British Library Cataloguing-in-Publication Data.
A catalogue record for this book is available from the British Library.

Published by Highland Books, an imprint of
Inter Publishing Service (IPS) Ltd,
St Nicholas House, 15 The Mount, Guildford, Surrey GU2 5HN.

Scripture quotations, unless otherwise noted, are taken from
The Good News Bible, the Bible in Today's English Version.
Copyright © American Bible Society 1966, 1971, 1976
published by Bible Societies/Collins and published in
Great Britain by the Bible Societies and Collins.

Printed in the UK by
HarperCollins Manufacturing, Glasgow

ISBN: 0 946616 11 6

Contents

II Advice Concerning Inward Things

III Conversations with God

IV Preparation for the Lord's Supper

Foreword

I first encountered *The Imitation of Christ* in 1947. Our pastor had given a copy to my brother as a high school graduation present. He never read it.

I tried to read it, but the English of the "revised translation" seemed archaic and virtually meaningless to my young mind. It may have been a treasure chest, but it was firmly locked and barred.

That little book found its way onto my shelves and followed me around until my forty-fourth year—a year of overwhelming stress and conflict.

At no other time in my life have I been more aware of my human frailty and my total dependence upon God. I had some tough professional decisions to make, values to sort out, priorities to establish, and responsibilities to shoulder. The time was ripe for me to discover personally the tremendous value of that little purple book I had been carrying around for more than thirty years. I had, by now, read widely enough so that the language was no longer a barrier to my understanding, and I had gained maturity enough for the concepts to make sense. To my astonishment, the thing lived and breathed! Day after day the messages of its brief chapters reached into the very heart of things, took the world as I had found it to be, and said something entirely rational and deeply spiritual about it. My own thinking was clarified and confirmed. I found in these pages wisdom and courage "for the facing of this hour . . . for the living of these days."

I read *The Imitation* under a variety of circumstances during the working day. I read it slowly, prayerfully. I marked it with a pencil, and copied portions of it to share with my wife. Sometimes, in my enthusiasm, I would telephone her and read a gem of a sentence I had just discovered. It was unbelievable how close the book's guidance came to my personal situation, how applicable its insights were to my professional dilemma. I can think of no better way to express it than to say that God met me in those pages. The prayers in the book prompted a profound inner response of prayer in myself. God and I *communicated*.

Sometimes I was so startled by what I had read, that I gave a little gasp of astonishment. How could anybody speak across all those centuries to my specific need with such clarity and certainty? These words were never intended for me; they were written by a monk to inspire and instruct those inside a monastery. And yet, the original author wrote with such genuine humanity, with such sincerity and insight into godliness, that the book has become the common possession of us all. It contains no barrier of time or place, no denominational narrowness. The words are sparks from the anvil of intense personal experience and they ignite spontaneous fires in the hearts of readers who recognize their own spiritual struggles. God, through these brief pages, has given us something pure and simple that drives straight to the heart of the only thing that really matters—our relationship with God and God's creation.

Such a discovery cries out to be shared. I highly recommended it to others. A few attempted to find in it what I had seen, but most could not seem to catch my enthusiasm. The available translations just didn't read easily enough for the average person in today's world. There were so many barriers of style to overcome. The book was like a black walnut: delicious meat concealed in a hard, unyielding shell.

I knew what my task was. After studying English translations and an edition in the original Latin, I began to rewrite, in my own language, certain pages of the great classic. To my delight, this process worked. There was nothing out of date in the author's understanding of people and God. All that was needed to make it accessible to modern readers was fresh expression. The task became a labor of love.

I should make it clear that you are not holding a literal translation of *De Imitatione Christi*. My purpose has been to communicate. I have tried to use language which clearly conveys the meaning and intent of the original while avoiding some of the traps inherent in a more literal rendering. For instance, when we are urged to have "contempt of ourselves," this is not an invitation to wallow in the depths of self-hatred and despair about ourselves, a thing alien to the life of Christ. Rather, the child of God is called upon to have a realistic estimation of himself as a person. What is meant by "contempt" in this case is something far more essential to the Christian life; I have called it, "a humble opinion of ourselves."

In Book I, Chapter XV, the author agrees with Seneca in saying that it is better to avoid society. "As often as I have been among men, I have returned home less a man." While seeing his point, I am not convinced that we see Christ demonstrate such an attitude. Jesus certainly escaped the crowds by retreating to lonely mountaintops, but only for brief periods. He did this in order to restore himself so that he could wade back into the masses to minister. Our Lord was at his best when in conversation with other people. In the same vein,

Chapter VIII encourages us to avoid social contact. "Don't converse too much with young people and strangers . . . Be friends with God and his angels, and avoid the acquaintance of men." All of this needs to be understood in the context of the book's original monastic setting, but it hardly offers Christian counsel today. I have, therefore, omitted these pages from the present edition.

The original audience was obviously male. For today's readers I have rendered such phrases as "My son," with the neuter, "My child." In places, I have paraphrased freely. In other places, I have omitted some of the original's parallelisms or dropped a repetitious paragraph. While this may result in a loss of some of the cumulative impact of reading *The Imitation* in its original form, the streamlining makes it move along faster for modern readers. Such editing has been done with care and discretion, and never with the intention of twisting this beautiful classic into a new shape.

The original contains a generous sprinkling of quotations from, and allusions to, Holy Scripture. I have allowed the allusions to pass without pointing them out. Direct quotations appear within quotation marks and are taken from the *Good News Bible (Today's English Version)*, published by the American Bible Society. In a few instances, where the original quotes only a fragment of a verse, I have included the entire verse.

The title of Thomas à Kempis's work has almost lost meaning to modern readers. Because the word turns up so frequently on supermarket shelves, "imitation" has come to mean "artificial." But the Latin, *imitatio*, means imitating or copying in the sense of *following* Christ. Of course, none of us can live a duplicate of the Perfect Life, but we can pattern our lives after Christ's in our own way. We know that Jesus Christ is far more than an excellent model for good living. He is the Son of God, our Savior. But once we have made that great affirmation of faith, we must begin inward growth that reflects our Lord's image. And it is in expressing the things we believe by the things we do that this little book offers its unsurpassed counsel.

Reading through these pages you will naturally want to know more about the origin and history of this Christian classic. (I've included background information in the Afterword to satisfy your curiosity.) In the five centuries of its existence it has appeared in about six thousand editions worldwide. Only the Bible has been translated into more languages. *The Imitation of Christ* has been read and appreciated by many of the greatest people in history, and by countless millions of less famous Christians and seekers—a number that continues to grow with each new generation. And now you are among them.

As you begin reading *The Imitation*, you step into a very special world, a world that seems curiously out of joint. The values it holds before us are not dear to a society based on selfish ambition. However, they may well be the perfect antidote to some of the poisonous ideas that currently infect our planet. Of this I have no doubt: the advice works. These pages are not merely quaint reminders of a bygone era. I believe the teachings were as radically opposed to popular values in the fourteenth century as they are to the values of today. Here is a human dynamic that remains forever true. When we are told where to find peace, or the route to misery, we are given an accurate road map, honestly labeled.

"There is a gentle eloquence in *The Imitation*," wrote Will Durant, "that echoes the profound simplicity of Christ's sermons and parables. It is an ever needed check on the intellectual pride of frail reason and shallow sophistication. When we are weary of facing our responsibilities in life we shall find no better refuge than Thomas à Kempis's Fifth Gospel."

PART I

VALUABLE ADVICE FOR SPIRITUAL LIVING

How to
Follow Christ
and Disregard
the World's
Prizes

The Lord says, "Whoever follows me will have the light of life and will never walk in darkness" (John 8:12). Christ encourages us to pattern our lives after his so we can become spiritually enlightened. Our most important task, then, is to meditate on the life of Jesus Christ.

Christ's teaching is superior to all the teachings of the saints, and if you have the Spirit you will discover through him "the hidden manna" of the Word (Rev. 2:17). Many who have heard the gospel all their lives have not been affected by it because they do not have Christ's Spirit. If you truly want to understand and enjoy the words of Christ, you must attempt to live like him.

What is the point of scholarly discussion of a deep subject like the Trinity, if you lack humility? You can be sure that profound talk does not make anyone holy and just, but a pure life pleases God. I would rather feel contrition than know its definition!

If you knew the entire Bible by heart and were familiar with all the philosophers, what good would it all be without the love of God and his grace?

Anything other than loving and serving God is "useless, useless . . . all useless" (Eccles. 1:2).

Here is the wisest thing you can do: forget the world and seek the things of heaven.

It is pointless, then, to desire and trust perishable wealth.

It is also pointless to search after honors or to be a social climber.

It is useless to give in to physical desires and to crave wrong things when indulging ourselves will only bring severe punishment.

It is futile to wish for a long life, and then to give so little care to living well.

It is nothing but vanity to think only of this present life and to ignore the future.

It is vain to care about things that are quickly passing away rather than to hurry to the place of everlasting joy.

Repeat this proverb frequently: "Our eyes can never see enough to be satisfied; our ears can never hear enough" (Eccles. 1:8). Try, then, to turn your heart away from the love of things that can be seen, and to start loving the things that cannot be seen. Those who follow the way of sensuality will have a nagging conscience and lose God's favor.

Have
a Humble
Opinion
of Yourself

It is natural for all of us to desire knowledge, but what is the value of knowledge without respect for God? The most ordinary person who serves God is better than a proud philosopher who neglects himself while studying the stars. If you really know yourself, you will see that nothing about yourself is worthy of praise. "I may have all knowledge and understand all secrets . . . but if I have no love, I am nothing" (1 Cor. 13:2). When I stand in God's presence, I am judged by the things I do.

Great learning can be a distraction; it can make you try to appear wise in order to win praise. There are many things you can know which will be of little value to your soul, and it is not wise to waste your time on them. Words do not nourish the soul, but a life well-lived brings comfort to the mind. A clear conscience will give you confidence before God.

If you think you know a lot about something, remind yourself that there are many more things you do not know. "Do not be proud, but accept humble duties. Do not think of yourselves as wise" (Rom. 12:16). If you want to learn something worthwhile, learn how to be a nobody.

The most profound and valuable lesson of all is to truly know yourself and to have a humble opinion of yourself.

Think well of others. If you see someone else engaging in a sinful act or a crime, do not let that make you think more highly of yourself. You do not know how long it may be before you also stumble. All of us are frail; consider yourself no stronger than anybody else!

True
Education

Lord, how happy is the person you instruct, the one to whom you teach your law!" (Ps. 94:12).

Our opinions and senses frequently mislead us. "What do we gain from all our work? . . . He has given us a desire to know the future, but never gives us the satisfaction of fully understanding what he does" (Eccles. 3:9, 11). We won't be held responsible for this ignorance.

O God of truth, unite me with yourself in everlasting love. I am tired of reading and hearing many things. All I desire is you. Silence all teachers. Let every creature be hushed reverently in your presence. Speak to me intimately.

The more a person is in harmony with himself and the more simple he is inwardly, the more he understands intuitively. He receives divine illumination.

A pure, honest, and stable spirit is not distracted by a lot of activity. He does everything to honor God and is at rest within himself. He seeks to be free from all selfishness.

A good, devout person considers inwardly the things he intends to do outwardly. Who has a greater struggle than one who tries to overcome himself? And this is our job—to work at conquering ourselves, to become stronger each day, and to make a little progress toward goodness.

Even our best efforts have imperfections, and all of our thinking includes some stupidity. A humble understanding of ourselves is a more certain way to God than the most indepth study.

But learning is not to be condemned! Knowledge is good. It is God's gift to us. However, a clear conscience and a decent life are superior to it. The fruitless error comes in desiring to know much, rather than to live well.

If we were as careful in weeding out vices and planting virtues as we are in scholarly research, we would not have so much evil and scandal among us, or so much carelessness in religious houses.

You can be certain of this: when the Day of Judgment comes, we shall not be asked what we have read, but what we have done; not how well we have spoken, but how well we have lived.

Tell me, where now are all the great doctors and masters you used to know? Others sit in their offices, and the former ones already are forgotten. See how soon this world's glory fades!

Authentic greatness is found in great love.

He is genuinely great who considers himself small, and cares nothing about high honors.

I am truly wise if I look upon all earthly things "as mere [garbage], so that I may gain Christ" (Phil. 3:8).

And the most learned of all is he that does the will of God while denying himself.

Prudent
Living

We should not be too credulous. We need to carefully consider everything we hear. We should spend time in thought before God. Sadly, we are so weak that we frequently believe and repeat ugly rumors rather than good things. It is best not to accept every report. Human beings have a tendency to evil, and even the most reliable sources make mistakes.

"Enthusiasm without knowledge is not good; impatience will get you into trouble" (Prov. 19:2). In a similar manner, don't believe everything you hear. Don't be quick to pour it into others' ears.

The more humility you have and the more subject you are to God, the wiser you will be, and the more at peace.

Reading
the
Bible

Look for truth in the Bible; not eloquence. Every verse should be read in the spirit with which it was written.

Read the devout and simple books as gladly as the learned and profound. Don't worry about the writer's authority, or his level of education. Allow the love of simple truth to attract you. Don't ask, "Who said this?" Instead, pay attention to what is said. People die, but God's Word will never pass away.

Sometimes our curiosity interferes with our Bible reading. We want to discuss and understand parts we should simply pass by.

If you want to make your Scripture reading worthwhile, read with humility, simplicity, and faith. Don't try to appear learned. Listen in silence to the words of the holy men, and take pleasure in the teachings of the elders. They spoke with good reason.

Controlling
Excess
Desire

If you want something obsessively, you will be restless within yourself. The arrogant and the greedy can never relax. It is the poor and the spiritually humble who know what peace is.

If you are not yet able to deny yourself, you will be easily tempted. Small, insignificant things will make you their slave.

The spiritually weak prefer sensuality and are not able to give up earthly desires completely. That's why they are sad when they must abandon something and easily angered when opposed.

Suppose you get something you want. Soon you may be remorseful to have that thing. Surrendering to your passions will not help you find peace. Only by resisting them can you be truly at peace.

There is simply no peace in the heart of a person who lives an animal existence or who places all importance on outward things. Peace is reserved for the sincerely spiritual person.

Taking
Charge

Be free! Master yourself! Make sure that all things are under you, and that you are not under them. Don't be a slave to anything. Be free!

Pride
and
Humility

The Lord says, 'I will condemn the person who turns away from me and puts his trust in man, in the strength of mortal man' " (Jer. 17:5).

Do not be ashamed to serve others because of your love for Jesus Christ, or to appear poor in the world's eyes.

Do not count on your own strength; trust God. Do what you can, and God will supply the difference.

"Wise men should not boast of their wisdom, nor strong men of their strength, nor rich men of their wealth" (Jer. 9:23).

"You must put on the apron of humility, to serve

one another; for the scripture says, 'God resists the proud, but shows favor to the humble'" (1 Pet. 5:5).

Take glory neither in money, if you have some, nor in influential friends, but in God who gives you everything and above all wants to give you himself.

Avoid boasting about the size or beauty of your body, which a little illness can disfigure or destroy.

Have no pride in your native wit and talent; that would displease God who gave you every good thing that you naturally possess.

Reject the thought that you are better than anyone else. If you think such haughty thoughts, God (who knows what is in you) will consider you worse than they.

Pride about our good deeds is pointless. God has his own ideas regarding what is good and he does not always agree with us. If there is anything good about you, believe better things of others. This will keep you humble.

It will not hurt you at all to consider yourself less righteous than others, but it will be disastrous for you to consider yourself better than even one person.

The humble are always at peace; the proud are often envious and angry.

Subjection
in the
Lord

It is of great importance to be obedient, to respect authority and to let someone else captain our ship. It is far safer to follow than to lead.

Yes, most people want to manage things their own way. But if God is among us, it is sometimes necessary to surrender our personal opinion in order to keep harmony.

Who is intelligent enough to know everything? Don't be too sure of yourself. Be willing to hear what others think. Sometimes, even if you have a good idea, it is better to discard it in favor of another, for God's sake. It is less dangerous to take advice than to give it.

Perhaps your opinion is just as good as anyone's. But if you stubbornly refuse to yield to others when there is a good reason or a just cause to do so, all you prove is your obstinate pride.

Guarding
the
Mouth

Avoid small talk as much as you can. Even shop talk can be a great hindrance. Sometimes I wish I had remained silent; that I had not spoken in a crowd.

Our chattering is an escape from unwelcome thinking. We keep the conversation on comfortable subjects. Small comfort! Sometimes it even robs us of inward consolation.

Watch and pray, so that you won't waste your time. If you want to talk about something, discuss a worthwhile subject.

Failing to guard your mouth is a very bad habit. But reverent discussion of spiritual matters can help us all grow, especially when the group that is gathered is unified in God.

Finding
Peace

—————————

We will have much peace if we refrain from minding the business of others.

Those with a unity of purpose are blessed with such peace.

Do you know why some of the saints were so genuine and contemplative? It was because they worked hard at being free from earthly desires. This allowed them to move closer to God and to develop their inner life freely.

We are enslaved too much by our emotions, and we worry too much about transitory things.

Only occasionally do we win out over even one vice, and no desire burns within us to improve daily the quality of our behavior. That is why we continue to be apathetic and cold. If we could overcome ourselves, and not be all mixed-up in our hearts, then we would be delighted with spiritual things and have a little experience with heavenly contemplation.

Our main problem—our *only* problem—is that we are caught in a spider's web of passions and lusts, and have no desire for a higher way. When even a minor problem comes up, we are immediately discouraged and turn to earthly kinds of comforts.

But if we try to be brave and stand firm in the battle, God certainly will help us. He presents us with the challenge and stands ready to assist us. All we need to do is trust his free gift of grace and we will win.

We would be well on the way to perfection if we could weed out one vice from ourselves each year. But we often find that we were better persons just after our conversion than we are after many years of being a Christian. Every day that passes should make us more like Christ, but we tend to grow cooler rather than warmer.

If we would make big demands on ourselves at the beginning, we would find it easier going later on. It is a hard job to quit old habits, and it is even more difficult to resist our own desires. But if you can't handle small things, how will you deal with big ones?

Put up a fight right at the beginning. Break a bad habit. Otherwise, it may draw you by small steps you never notice into greater difficulty.

If you had any idea how much inward peace you would gain for yourself, and how much joy you would bring to others, by devoting yourself singleheartedly to God, you would certainly pay more attention to your spiritual progress.

The Value
of Adversity

Sometimes it is good for us to have trouble and crosses to bear. Adversity can return us to our senses. It can remind us that we are here as refugees, and that we must not place our trust in anything belonging to the world.

It is good that people sometimes misunderstand us, that they have a poor opinion of us even when our intentions are good. Such experiences lead us toward humility and protect us from conceit. Under trying circumstances we seek God all the more. Our inner life grows stronger when we are outwardly condemned.

If you will fully establish yourself in God, you will not need the consolation of others. When we are troubled with temptation and evil thoughts, then we see clearly the great need we have of God, since without him we can do nothing good. Then with weariness and sorrow we may "want very much to leave this life and be with Christ" (Phil. 1:23), for we understand that absolute security and peace do not exist in this world.

How to Resist Temptation

As long as we live in this world, we will endure trials and temptation. As it is written in Job,

"Human life is like forced army service,
like a life of hard manual labor,
like a slave longing for cool shade;
like a worker waiting for his pay" (Job 7:1-2).

Be careful, therefore, about your own temptations. Pray about them. "Be alert, be on the watch! Your enemy, the Devil, roams around like a roaring lion, looking for someone to devour" (1 Pet. 5:8). No one is so good that he is immune to temptation; we will never be entirely free of it.

Still, temptation can be a service to us. It may be a burden, but it can bring us humility and teach us good lessons. All of the saints experienced more than their share of trials and temptations, and they grew as a result.

There is no group so holy, no place so far away, that it can shield us from all distractions and difficulties. No one living on earth is entirely free from temptation. The reason is that we are born with the source of temptation within us; we are trapped by our own evil desire.

We are fallen men living east of Eden. Therefore tribulation will never leave us and one temptation will always follow on the heels of another.

Many people try to run away from temptations only to fall even harder. Trying to escape is not the solution. What makes us stronger than any of our enemies is patience and humility. If you only try to avoid temptations outwardly (rather than pluck them out by the roots) you will not get very far. Like weeds in a poorly cultivated garden, they will soon return worse than before.

Gradually, by patience and persistence, with God's help, you will win a victory that could never be yours through the violence of your own fretful efforts.

Seek counsel when you are tempted, and don't be hard on someone else who is tempted. Give him the same loving support you would want for yourself.

Two things increase temptation's hold on you: an indecisive mind and little confidence in God. As a ship without a rudder is driven this way and that by the tossing waves, so the careless and irresolute person is battered by temptations on every side.

Fire tests iron; temptation tests an honest person. Sometimes we don't know what we can do until temptation shows us what we are.

But don't play with fire! It is far easier to deal successfully with temptation in the beginning, when the flames are still controllable. The time to deal with the enemy is while he remains outside the door of your heart. Take him on as soon as you hear the first knock. As Ovid said, "Prevent the illness; medicine comes too late."

First a mere thought comes to mind;

then a strong imagination works on it.
Pleasure may come,
followed by a tendency to evil,
and suddenly, we are hooked.

Little by little the enemy takes over because we let him get his foot in the door. The longer we put off resisting, the weaker we become.

Some people are tempted most strongly at the beginning of their spiritual life, others near the end. Some are troubled all their lives. Still others receive only light temptation. Such things are decided by God and we can trust his wisdom.

Therefore, we must not despair when we are tempted. Instead, we must pray to God all the more sincerely, asking him to help. Saint Paul has assured us, "Every test that you have experienced is the kind that normally comes to people. But God keeps his promise, and he will not allow you to be tested beyond your power to remain firm; at the time you are put to the test, he will give you the strength to endure it, and so provide you with a way out" (1 Cor. 10:13).

"Humble yourselves, then, under God's mighty hand" (1 Pet. 5:6) in all temptation and difficulty, for he will save and honor those who are humble in spirit. It is no great accomplishment to be devout and fervent when your life is running smoothly, but patient endurance in troubled times is strong confirmation of your growth in grace.

Some are spared great temptations, only to be trapped by little ones each day. Being weak in small things, they never receive the big assignments.

Passing
Judgment

T ake a good look at yourself; don't judge what others do. Your evaluation of someone else will often be mistaken, but you can be fruitfully honest with yourself.

Living with
Imperfections
in Others

T ry to be patient with the defects and blemishes in others, because you also have many things about you that they must endure. If you can't make yourself what you want to be, how can you expect to remake somebody else?

We would like to see another person perfect, and yet we ignore our own faults. We would be pleased if others were severely corrected, but we are reluctant to accept similar treatment for ourselves. We want the law to apply to everybody but ourselves. It is clear that we don't measure our neighbors and ourselves by the same standard.

If everyone were perfect, there would be nothing in others for us to bear with for God's sake. But God has seen to it that we must "help to carry one another's burdens" (Gal. 6:2).

For no one is without fault,
no one is without burden,
no one is self-sufficient,
no one is wise enough on his own.

Therefore, we must support one another, comfort one another, help, teach, and caution one another.

Peace
Does Not
Come from
Others

Friend, if you expect to find peace in the friendship of any person, you are likely to be disappointed. But if you are intimate with God, the disloyalty or death of a friend will not crush you. Base your love for your friend on God, for without him, friendship is weak and won't last. Love that is bonded together by God is pure and true.

Life
in a
Monastery

You must learn how to overcome many of your own desires if you want to live peacefully and in harmony with others. It is a great accomplishment to live in a religious community, or be a part of a congregation, without complaining, and to stick with it faithfully until you die.

You must be willing to seem a fool for Christ's sake if you want to live a religious life.

Wearing special clothes and shaving your head contribute almost nothing to your spiritual life, but changing your behavior and controlling your emotions make you truly religious.

If you pursue anything other than God and the salvation of your soul, you will find trouble and sorrow.

You will not have peace unless you try to be the least, subordinate to all.

You came here to serve, not to rule. Now it is your duty to endure difficulties tolerantly and to work, not to rest idly and waste time in small talk.

Here, we are tested as gold in the furnace. Here, no one can stand the test—unless he is willing with all his heart to be humble before God.

Compare Yourself with Early Christians

Consider the early Christians' shining examples of faithfulness, and you will see how little we do. There is no comparison!

The saints and followers of Christ served the Lord in hunger and thirst, in cold and nakedness, in toil and weariness, in observances and fasts, in prayer and holy meditation, in persecution and disgrace.

All day long they labored, and at night they prayed continually. Even at work, they prayed silently.

Every hour they spent with God seemed short. They enjoyed this communion so much they sometimes forgot to eat.

They were strangers to the world, but they were God's close companions.

After you have seen such examples of faith, it will be difficult for you to fall asleep spiritually.

Essentials
for
Each Day

A Christian ought to be as virtuous inside as he appears outside to others. No, he should be *better* in his heart than on the surface. Because God sees every part of us, we should be reverent before him and live as pure as angels in his sight.

We should pray every day, saying, "Help me, O Lord God! These are my good intentions in your service. Let me begin this day to settle down to the serious business of living a pure life, for what I have done so far is nothing."

The firmer we stick to our purpose, the more we will advance. And if the one who tries the hardest frequently fails, what will become of the less enthusiastic? Remember that our best intentions do not depend upon us for fulfillment, but upon God. We are to rely on him for whatever we try to do. "You may make your plans, but God directs your actions" (Prov. 16:9).

Even if we do the best we can, we will still fail many times. Yet we must always plan something definite, plot a course, especially as we battle our greatest personal weaknesses.

Determine a plan of action in the morning, and then evaluate yourself at night. How have you behaved today? What were your words, your deeds, your thoughts? It may be that you have offended

God or your neighbor.

Never be completely at rest. Read, or write, or pray, or meditate, or do something good for the community.

Everyone cannot profit from the same kind of spiritual practices; one is better for you, and another is better for someone else. In the same way we must choose spiritual practices that suit the occasion. There are different ways for dealing with holidays and regular days, temptation and peace, sadness and happiness.

The point is that we should prepare ourselves for a good departure from this earth.

"How happy that servant is," says the gospel writer, Luke, "if his master finds him doing this when he comes home! Indeed, I tell you, the master will put that servant in charge of all his property" (Luke 12:43-44).

Enjoy
Being Alone
and Quiet

Watch for good times to retreat into yourself. Frequently meditate on how good God is to you. Skip the tricky questions. Read things which will move your heart.

If you will stop chattering and gossiping, you will find plenty of time for valuable meditation.

You will find in your "closet of prayer" what you frequently lose when you are out in the world. The more you visit it, the more you will want to return. But the longer you avoid it, the harder it will be to come back. If you are faithful to your secret place, it will become your closest friend and bring you much comfort. In silence and stillness, a devout person grows spiritually and learns the hidden things of the Bible. The tears shed there bring cleansing. God will draw near the person who withdraws for a while.

It is better for you to look after yourself this way in private than to perform wonders in public while neglecting your soul.

Turn to God Almighty. Ask him to forgive your sins and oversights. Leave trivial things to the trivial. "Go to your room, close the door" (Matt. 6:6), and speak with Jesus, your Beloved. Stay there with him. Nowhere else will you find this kind of peace.

Dealing with
Malicious
Gossip

_____

Friend, stay near God and don't worry about what others think of you when you have a clear conscience. It is a good thing to suffer such misjudgment. If you are humble, it won't even bother you. Many people say things that are not worth hearing.

It is impossible to satisfy everyone. Paul became "all things to all men" (1 Cor. 9:22). And yet he said, "I am not at all concerned about being judged by you or by any human standard; I don't even pass judgment on myself" (1 Cor. 4:3). He did everything he could to lead others to Christ, but he still had plenty of detractors. This is how Paul preserved his sanity: he turned it all over to God who knows everything. When necessary, Paul faced those who tried to raise their own status by climbing over him. He answered their charges with humility and patience in order to protect others who might be hurt by his silence.

"The Lord says,
I am the one who strengthens you.
Why should you fear mortal man, who is no
more enduring than grass?" (Isa. 51:12).

What power does anyone have to injure you with words? He hurts himself, not you. And he will be unable to escape God's judgment, regardless of who he is. Keep God in sight and ignore others' abuse.

Understanding
Human
Misery

You will suffer, wherever you are, unless you are with God.

Why are you upset when things don't go the way you wish? Who gets everything his way? I don't. You don't. No one does. Not one person on earth—not even a king or a pope—has a problem-free life. Do you know who can deal with troubles best? It is the person who is willing to suffer something for God.

Thoughtless people say, "Look at the happy life that person leads! Money! Prestige! Power!" But if you consider the riches of heaven, you will see that these earthly things are inconsequential, undependable, and more a burden than a privilege. They are always accompanied by anxiety and fear. Our happiness does not depend upon owning a lot of things; enough to get along will do.

Life on earth involves misery. The spiritually perceptive person is even more aware of this because he sees clearly the effects of human corruption.

For that matter, to eat and drink, to sleep and wake, to work and rest, and to be forced to obey the other requirements of nature can become a great annoyance to a devout person who would almost prefer to live without a body!

Friend, don't give up your spiritual journey. You still have time. Why do you keep putting off your decision day after day? You can start immediately. You can say, "This is the moment to start moving. Now is the time to begin the fight and to change my ways."

How great is our weakness of character! Today you will confess your sins; tomorrow you will commit the same ones again. Right now, you intend to do better. In an hour, you will behave as though this moment never happened.

We have every reason, therefore, to be humble— we are so weak and unstable.

Thinking
About
Death

You won't last long here. Think about what will become of you in another world. You are here today and gone tomorrow.

How sad is the dullness and hardness of our hearts! We only think about the present and have little concern for what is to come.

Instead, we should plan every word and action as though we were going to die today. If you had a clean conscience you would not be afraid to die. It is better to run away from sin than from death. If you are not ready for death today, do you think you will be any more prepared tomorrow? Tomorrow is not guaranteed. How can you be sure you'll even live until tomorrow?

Living a long time doesn't make us better persons automatically. Sometimes the years increase only our burden of guilt, not the quality of our behavior. It would be wonderful if we could live even one day well. Many can tell you the date of their conversion, but their lives have little to show for it.

The person who thinks about his own death and daily prepares to die will be blessed. If you ever watch another person die, remember that you must also pass the same way. When morning comes, think that you will not live until sunset. At night, don't promise yourself a morning. Always be ready. Live in such a way that death will never catch you unprepared. "You must always be ready, because the Son of Man will come at an hour when you are not expecting him" (Matt. 24:44).

When your last hour comes, you will have a new perspective on your entire life, and you will be deeply troubled if you have been careless and negligent.

"Listen! This is the hour to receive God's favor; today is the day to be saved!" (2 Cor. 6:2). The time will come when you will beg for one day or one hour to make amends, and you may not be granted it.

Try to live now so that when your time comes to die, you will be glad rather than afraid. Discover how to die to the world so you can start living with Christ.

It is foolish to think that you will have a long life. You can't even be sure you will get through today! Many have been snatched suddenly out of this world. Think of the times you have heard of someone drowning, or choking to death, or dying while playing a sport. Fire, weapons, sickness, violent thieves—these unexpected threats are constantly present with us. "We grow and wither as quickly as flowers; we disappear like shadows" (Job 14:2).

Do it now. Do whatever you can do right now. You never know when your opportunity will be ended by death. While you have the time, start collecting heavenly treasures. Think about nothing but your spiritual health. Care about nothing but the things of God.

Live as a stranger and a refugee in this world—
as one who has nothing to do with earthly things.
Keep your heart free and lifted up to God, "for
there is no permanent city for us here on earth; we
are looking for the city which is to come" (Heb.
13:14). That is where to send your prayers, sighs,
and tears. Then, when you die, your spirit will be
joyfully at home with Christ.

Divine
Judgment

Always consider the end—how you will
stand before God, your judge, from whom nothing
can be kept secret. He cannot be bribed, and will
not be deceived by flimsy excuses, but will certainly judge you honestly. If you are sometimes disturbed by the expression on an angry person's face,
how will you feel before God, who knows everything about your foolish and sinful life? The time to
do your weeping and pleading is *now,* while it can
still accomplish good for you and in you.

Here is the picture of a patient and purifying life:
*Though you receive injuries, you are more troubled
by the other's malice than by any wrong done to you.*

You willingly pray for your enemies, and sincerely forgive them. If you have offended or hurt someone else, you are quick to ask for pardon.

Compassion is stronger in you than anger.

You passionately overcome your own will in order to subdue your body to your spirit.

It is better to eliminate sinful behavior here than to deal with it hereafter. What fuel shall the fires have but your sins?

There is no future in anything, then, except loving and serving God. If you love God with all your heart, you will not be afraid of death, or punishment, or judgment, or hell. Perfect love brings divine security. But if that love is not yet strong enough in you to keep you from sinning, then maybe the fear of hell will restrain you.

Good Advice for Good Living

Trust in the Lord and do good;
live in the land and be safe.
Seek your happiness in the Lord,
and he will give you your heart's desire.
Give yourself to the Lord;

trust in him, and he will help you" (Ps. 37:3-5).

Carefully avoid in yourself those things which disturb you in others.

Pick some profitable fruit wherever you are. If you see or hear a good example, burn the imitation of it into your soul. But if you observe behavior that is harmful, avoid it like a snake. And if you already have committed the same sin yourself, get busy and make amends. Just as you observe others' actions, they observe yours.

You will always be glad at night, if you have lived the day fruitfully. Cautiously watch yourself. Whatever happens to others, don't neglect your own spiritual life.

PART II

ADVICE CONCERNING
INWARD THINGS

The
Inner Life

The kingdom of God is within you," says the Lord (Luke 17:21). Turn wholeheartedly to God, give up this miserable world, and you will discover rest for your soul. Learn to scorn outward things; concentrate on what goes on inside yourself. If you do, you will see the Kingdom of God come to you. "For God's kingdom is not a matter of eating and drinking, but of the righteousness, peace, and joy which the Holy Spirit gives" (Rom. 14:17). And that is not given to vicious people.

Christ will come to you, bringing his special consolation with him, if you prepare a worthy place for him within yourself. The glory and beauty of Christ is an inner thing. He enjoys frequent visits quietly inside you. His conversation is deliciously pleasant; his comfort and peace are tremendous. It is marvelous to be his familiar friend.

Prepare yourself, faithful soul, to welcome your lover, that he may come to you and live with you as your spouse. This is what he says, "Whoever accepts my commandments and obeys them is the one who loves me. My father will love whoever loves me; I too will love him and reveal myself to him" (John 14:21).

When you have Christ, you are rich. He is enough. He will provide everything you need so you won't have to count on others without him. People change and fail. You cannot depend upon them. Those that are for you today may be against you tomorrow. They are as variable as the wind. But Christ is eternally faithful.

Put all of your trust in God. Reverently love him. He will look out for you. "For there is no permanent city for us here on earth; we are looking for the city which is to come" (Heb. 13:14). Wherever you may be, you are a stranger and a pilgrim. You will never really rest until you are united inwardly with Christ. Why are you looking around for a resting place here? This is not your home; heaven is. Everything here is transitory, and you are no exception.

If you need help in learning how to meditate on

high and heavenly things, think about Christ's will-
ingness to die on the cross. Live for a while in his
sacred wounds. This will bring you great comfort
in tribulation, and will take the sting out of any
trouble the world sends your way. Christ was in the
world just as you are. He was despised and rejected, and his best friends deserted him when he was
in deep trouble.

Christ was willing to suffer; do you dare to complain? Christ had enemies and detractors; so you
want everyone to be your friend and benefactor?

There is no way your patience can receive a
heavenly crown if you face no earthly problems. If
you will not accept any opposition, how will you
be Christ's friend? If even once you have truly discovered the secrets of the Lord Jesus, and tasted a
sample of his great love, then you will not care two
cents for your own convenience or inconvenience.

A lover of Jesus and of the Truth, a genuinely
sincere Christian who is free from encumbering
desires, can spontaneously turn to God, lift himself
above himself spiritually, and fruitfully linger there.

If you can evaluate things as they really are, and
not as people report them to be, then you are wise,
and God is your teacher.

Humility

Don't pay much attention to who is for you and who is against you. This is your major concern: that God be with you in everything you do. If you have a good conscience, God will be your defender and no man can hurt you. If you can suffer silently, you will see how the Lord can help. God knows when and how to rescue you. Trust him.

It can be helpful for others to know our faults and blame us for them. Such experiences keep us humble, and humility goes a long way toward reconciling us to others.

God protects and helps the humble; he loves and comforts them.

He notices their humility; he pours out his grace on them.

When a humble one has been cast down, God raises him to glory.

He tells his secrets to the humble.

He draws them by invitation to himself.

If you are humble, you will be at peace even while experiencing shame, because your foundation is God and not the world. Don't think that you have made any progress at all, until you see less virtue in yourself than in anybody else.

It Is Good to Be Peaceable

If you are at peace yourself, then you will be able to help others become peaceable. An excitable person distorts things, and readily believes the worst, but a calm person can turn even bad circumstances into good ones. If you are at peace, you will not be suspicious of others. But if you are discontented and troubled, you will be agitated with all kinds of suspicions. You will be unable to remain quiet yourself, and you will not let anyone else rest either.

Accuse yourself and excuse another. See how far you are from genuine love and humility, which do not know how to be angry or indignant toward anyone else. It is no significant accomplishment to live with good and gentle people. Everybody enjoys compatible company! But to be able to get along with obstinate, disorderly, and contrary people is a unique gift, a highly commendable feat.

The person who knows best how to suffer will enjoy the most peace. Such a person has conquered himself and has become a lord of the world, a friend of Christ, and an inheritor of heaven.

Simplicity
and
Purity

These two wings will lift you high above earthly things: simplicity and purity. Simplicity of intention is after God's own heart; purity of affection sees him and tastes him. If you intend to look for nothing but the will of God and the good of your neighbor, you will enjoy abundant inner freedom.

If your soul is healthy, then every creature you see will be a living mirror, a book of sacred doctrine. There is no creature, regardless of its apparent insignificance, that fails to show us something of God's goodness. If you were inwardly good and pure, you would be able to comprehend everything easily. An unblemished heart penetrates heaven and hell.

What you are inside will color your judgment. If there is joy in this world, it is the pure in heart who experience it. And if there is suffering and anguish anywhere, it is all too familiar to the bad conscience.

As iron put into a fire loses its rust and glows red in the heat, so the one who turns completely to God, wakes up and becomes a new person. It is when you begin to cool that you start fearing any little demand made of you, and you seek escape in earthly ways. But when, with God's help, you begin to gain control of yourself, you will pay little attention to things that used to bother you deeply.

What Comes Naturally—and What Is a Gift from God

Don't be fooled by what only appears to be good. Human nature and grace move in opposite directions. Here is how to tell the difference between the two.

Human nature is tricky and often misleads and traps; it always cares about itself. But grace simply avoids guile and cares about God.

Human nature puts up a fight and dies reluctantly; it is not easily taught new patterns or held under control. Grace avoids sensuality, desires to be held in check, and will not abuse freedoms.

Human nature always works for its own profit and advantage and seeks all it can gain from others. Grace does not think at all about itself, but instead about what is good for others.

Human nature accepts flattery, honor, and adulation gladly. Grace passes on the honor and worship to God.

Human nature hates to be shamed or rejected, but grace is pleased to endure such things in the name of God and accepts them as special favors when they come.

Human nature desires exotic and exclusive things. But grace enjoys the ordinary, and is willing to be dressed in simple clothes.

Human nature is greedy and finds receiving more blessed than giving. It enjoys owning private property. But grace is generous to the poor and content with a little. It knows "there is more happiness in giving than in receiving" (Acts 20:35).

Human nature does nothing because of generosity. Its constant aim is to gain the advantage. It wants praise and notoriety. But grace looks for no rewards beyond God and cares nothing for empty applause.

Human nature desires to have many friends and relatives and takes pride in its pedigree. It enjoys being among rich and important people. But grace loves its enemies and places virtue above noble birth. It sympathizes more with the innocent than with the influential, and finds truth more impressive than propaganda.

Human nature wants recognition. It wants admiration for good deeds. But grace hides its good works and private devotion and gives all praise to God.

Such grace is a heavenly light, a gift from God. It

is the mark of a truly spiritual person. As nature is restrained, grace increases, and the soul becomes stamped with the image of God.

How to Think of Yourself

Don't trust your own judgment about yourself. We usually lack the grace or understanding to see clearly. The little light that is in us is quickly lost because of our negligence. Our spiritual vision is poorer than we realize. We frequently do something wrong, and then make it worse with excuses. Sometimes we are motivated by uncontrollable emotion and consider it "righteous indignation." We direct attention to small flaws in others while disregarding far worse things in ourselves. We carefully count others' offenses against us, but we rarely consider what others may suffer because of us. If we look at ourselves honestly, we will judge others less harshly.

If you are a genuine Christian, you will look for your own faults first, and you will keep silent about others' shortcomings. If you are totally absorbed in your personal relationship with God, you won't meddle in other lives.

Where are you when you are not with yourself? And when you have been everywhere and examined everybody else, what good will it do if you have neglected yourself?

If you want peace and unity of purpose, then you must put everything else out of sight. You will fail miserably if you value anything material. Let nothing be important for you, nothing high, nothing pleasant, nothing acceptable, unless it is simply God, or something that pleases God. Think of creature comforts as a waste of energy. A soul that loves God is not satisfied with anything less than God. God alone is eternal, infinite, present everywhere. He alone can comfort the soul and make the heart glad.

The Joy of a Clean Conscience

The glory of a good person is the evidence of a clean conscience. Keep your conscience clear and you will be happy. A good conscience is able to bear a heavy load and it will encourage you when you are under attack. A bad conscience is always afraid and uneasy.

Your sleep will be sweet if your heart does not accuse you.

Scoundrels are never really happy. They have no peace. "There is no safety for sinners, says the Lord" (Isa. 48:22).

And if they say, "No harm will come to us," don't believe them. God's wrath will one day surprise them, and their works and ideas will perish.

The praise of the world is short-lived and always accompanied by sorrow. The glory of the good is in their consciences, not in the comments of others.

Anyone who goes looking for stardom and does not count fame unimportant reveals little fondness for heavenly things. The most tranquil person of all is the one who cares about neither the praise nor the fault-finding of others. You are not a better person because you are praised; neither are you any worse if somebody denigrates you. You are what you are. Words can't change that. God knows what you are. If you really get to know your inner self, you won't care what anyone says about you. People consider actions, but God evaluates intentions.

If you are not looking for stardom, you have clearly committed yourself to God, "For it is when the Lord thinks well of a person that he is really approved, and not when he thinks well of himself" (2 Cor. 10:18).

To be God's close friend, and not to be a slave to any earthly desire, is the mark of a spiritual person.

Loving Jesus
Comes First

Happiness comes to the person who knows how to love Jesus and to disregard himself for Christ's sake. Our love for Jesus must exceed all other loves. Love the world and you will collapse when it collapses; embrace Jesus and you will have stability forever.

Love him. Keep him as a friend. When all others forsake you, he will remain faithful to the end.

Eventually whether you choose it or not, you will be separated from everyone else. Therefore, stay close to Jesus in both life and death. Trust his fidelity. When all others fail, he alone can help you.

It is your Beloved's nature to desire no rivals, to ask for your full devotion.

If you look for Jesus in all things, you will certainly find him. And if you look only for yourself, you will find only yourself, but it will be your loss. Those who do not seek Jesus bring more harm on themselves than all their enemies could ever inflict.

How to Be Christ's Close Friend

When Jesus is with us, all is well and nothing seems insurmountable. But when Jesus is absent, everything is difficult. If Jesus does not speak to us inwardly, all other comfort is meaningless. But the slightest communication from him brings consolation. Recall how Mary Magdalene immediately stopped crying when Martha said to her, "The Teacher is here, and is asking for you" (John 11:28). It is a delightful moment when Jesus calls us from tears to spiritual joy!

Life without Jesus is like a dry garden baking in the sun. It is foolish to want anything that conflicts with Jesus. What can the world give you without Jesus? His absence is hell; his presence, paradise. If Jesus is with you, no enemy can injure you. Whoever finds Jesus has discovered a great treasure, the best of all possible good. The loss of him is a tremendous misfortune, more than the loss of the entire world. Poverty is life without Jesus, but close friendship with him is incalculable wealth.

We must develop our skill as carefully as an artist does if we want to live intimately with Jesus. Be humble and peaceable, and Jesus will be with you. Be devout and quiet, and Jesus will reside with you.

You may drive him out of your life if you return

to outward things. And if you should repel him, and lose him, where will you run to find a friend? Life is nothing without a friend, and if Jesus isn't your best friend you will be sad and lonely. It would be better to have the entire world against us rather than to offend Jesus.

Make many friends; love them dearly. But love Jesus in a special way. Love others because of Jesus, but love Jesus for himself. For him, and in him, love both your friends and your enemies. Pray for them all, asking God to lead them to know and love Jesus also. Never seek this kind of devoted love for yourself. Such devotion belongs to God alone.

If discouraging and unpleasant days come your way, don't be despondent or defeated. Stand strong in God and bear whatever you must to the glory of Jesus Christ. For after winter, summer comes; after night, the day returns; and after a storm, calm is restored.

When We
Can Find
No Comfort

It is not difficult to be independent of human comfort when we have God's comfort. It is a great thing, an *extremely* great thing, to be able to live without both human and divine comfort, to be willing to endure cheerfully an exile of the heart for the honor of God, to ask nothing for yourself, and to claim no special favors because of your good works.

Why should anyone be impressed if you are happy and faithful when everything is going your way? God's grace gives a smooth ride. It isn't surprising that you don't feel your burden if the Almighty is carrying it for you!

You must go through a long and tremendous conflict within yourself before you can begin to master yourself and give your heart to God.

Therefore, when God comforts you spiritually, receive it with gratitude. You can be sure it is his gift to you—you did not deserve it. Don't let that gift swell you with pride. Instead, accept it in all humility. And watch your step! That moment of comfort will also pass, and new temptations await you around the next corner.

If you should temporarily lose your sense of well-being, don't be too quick to despair. With humility and patience, wait for God who is able to give you back even more profound comfort.

There is nothing novel about this to those who are familiar with God's ways. The great saints and ancient prophets frequently experienced the alternation of up and down, joy and sorrow. One of them, while he was enjoying a mountain-top experience said:

'I felt secure and said to myself,
'I will never be defeated.'
You were good to me, Lord;
you protected me like a mountain fortress.
But then you hid yourself from me,
And I was afraid' (Ps. 30:6-7).

And yet, even while he was going through this, he did not feel crushed. With renewed passion he prayed:

'Hear me, Lord, and be merciful!
Help me, Lord!' (Ps. 30:10).

In time, his prayer was answered. This is his report:

'You have changed my sadness into a joyful dance;
you have taken away my sorrow
and surrounded me with joy' (Ps. 30:11).

If great saints are exposed to such variations, we who are poor and weak should not be discouraged if our spiritual life fails to be uniformly ecstatic. The Holy Spirit gives and takes according to his own divine purpose.

Where shall I place my hope and confidence except in God's great mercy? For whether I am in good company, or have with me faithful friends, or religious books, or beautiful writings, or sweet music, all of these are little help when God seems far from me and I am left alone in the poverty of my being.

I have never met anyone so religious and devout that he has not felt occasionally some withdrawing of grace, some decrease in his spiritual consciousness. No saint was ever so enraptured and inspired that he escaped temptation before and after the great moment. Anyone who has never suffered a little for God's sake is not worthy of deep spiritual contemplation.

Remember the promise of heavenly comfort: "To those who win the victory I will give the right to eat the fruit of the tree of life that grows in the Garden of God" (Rev. 2:7).

The Devil never sleeps, and your flesh is very much alive. Therefore, constantly prepare yourself for battle. Surrounding you are enemies that never rest.

Be Thankful
for God's
Grace

You were born to work; why are you looking for rest? Adjust yourself to patience rather than to comfort, and to bearing the Cross rather than to mirth.

It is good of God to comfort us with his love. But we do evil when we fail to return it all to God again with thanksgiving. Ingratitude can stop the flow of God's love in us.

I will refuse any sort of consolation that destroys my repentance, and I will shrink from anything that leads to pride. Not all that is high is holy; neither are all enjoyable things good. Not every desire is pure; neither is everything that we cherish pleasing to God.

If you are taught by the gift of grace, and instructed by the terrible loss of it, you will not dare to claim any goodness in yourself; rather, you will admit that you are poor and naked. Give God what is God's and take credit for what is your own. In other words, thank God for his kindness and blame yourself for your own sin and the punishment it brings.

Always take the lowest place, and the highest will be given to you, for high structures require a solid foundation. The greatest, in the judgment of God, are the least in their own opinion; the more worthy they are, the more humility will be seen in them. People who are filled with honesty and heavenly glory don't look for empty praise. Those who are grounded in God simply cannot be conceited. If they recognize God as the giver of every good thing they have ever received, they don't seek applause from each other. They desire more than anything else that God may be praised in them.

Be thankful, therefore, for the smallest gift; then you will be worthy to receive greater things. Accept the most insignificant present as though it were something of special value. If you consider the worth of the Giver, no gift will seem trivial or worthless. Nothing given by almighty God can be of small value. Yes, even if he sends pain or sorrow, we should thank him for it, because he is always thinking of our eternal good.

Only a Few Love the Cross

Jesus has many who love his heavenly kingdom, but few who bear his Cross. Many want consolation, but few desire adversity. Many are eager to share Jesus' table, but few will join him in fasting.

Everyone would be glad to rejoice with him, but not many are willing to suffer for him. Many will follow Jesus as far as the breaking of bread, but few will stay to drink the cup of his passionate self-sacrifice. Many are inspired by his miracles, but few accept the shame of his Cross. Many love Jesus as long as they have no troubles. Many praise and bless him as long as they receive some comfort from him. But if Jesus hides himself, leaving them even briefly, they start complaining and become dejected.

But those who love Jesus for Jesus' sake, and not for any special privileges, bless him in all difficulties and anguish, as well as in times of great comfort. Even if he should never comfort them again, they would continue to praise and thank him. What astonishing power rests in the pure love of Jesus which is not corrupted with self-interest or self-love! One term describes those who are always looking for comfort: *mercenary.* Don't they show themselves to be lovers of self rather than Christ? All they care about is their own advantage and profit.

Where can we find anyone who is willing to serve God for nothing? It is rare to discover someone so spiritual! Do you know anyone who is truly poor in spirit and free from dependence on any created thing? Such a person "is worth far more than jewels!" (Prov. 31:10).

"If anyone tried to buy love with his wealth, contempt is all he would get" (Song of Songs 8:7). And if someone tries hard to make amends for all of his sins, he still hasn't done very much. And if he receives the best education, he still has a long way to go. And if he is exceedingly virtuous and glowing with devotion, an essential ingredient is still lacking. What must he do? He must give up everything, especially himself, retaining no trace of selfishness. And when he has done everything required of him, he must consider it as nothing. He must not agree with others when they applaud him, but rather admit that he is actually an ordinary servant.

As the Gospel says, "When you have done all you have been told to do, say, 'We are ordinary servants; we have only done our duty'" (Luke 17:10). After admitting this he may be honestly poor in spirit, and may say with the psalmist, "Turn to me, Lord, and be merciful to me, because I am lonely and weak" (Ps. 25:16).

And yet, no one will be richer, no one more powerful, no one more free, because he is able to leave himself and all material things behind, and set himself in the lowest place.

The Royal Highway of the Holy Cross

Many have difficulty with these words: "If anyone wants to come with me, he must forget himself, carry his cross, and follow me" (Matt. 16:24). But they will find it even harder to hear that last statement: "Away from me, you that are under God's curse! Away to the eternal fire . . ." (Matt. 25:41).

Those who gladly hear and follow Christ shall have no reason to fear such a condemnation. Every servant of the Cross who has lived like the crucified Christ will face the heavenly Judge with confidence. Why, then, are you afraid to carry your cross when it leads you to such a kingdom?

In the Cross is salvation,
in the Cross is life,
in the Cross is protection from our enemies,
in the Cross is good mental health,
in the Cross is spiritual joy,
in the Cross is virtue at its best,
in the Cross is the full perfection of holiness.

There is no salvation of soul, nor hope of eternal life, except in the Cross. Carry your cross and follow Jesus. He went first, carrying his cross, and then dying on it for you. If you are dead with him, you will also live with him. And if you share his punishment, you will also share his glory. Look far and wide and still you will not find a better way above, or a safer way below, than the highway of the holy Cross.

Even if you use the best judgment and make the best plans, you will still find it necessary to suffer, willingly or unwillingly. There is no escaping the Cross. You will feel either pain in your body or tribulation in your spirit. Sometimes you will feel deserted by God. Sometimes your neighbor will trouble you. Quite frankly, you will sometimes be a burden to yourself. As long as God wants you to bear it, there can be no remedy for your suffering, because there are some vital lessons you need to learn. You must subject yourself entirely to God, and become more humble by the things you suffer. No one is better able to appreciate the Passion of Christ than the one who has suffered similarly.

The Cross, therefore, is inescapable. It waits for you everywhere. No matter how far you run, you cannot hide from it. For wherever you go, you take yourself along. Above and below, inside and outside, everywhere you turn, you shall find the Cross.

If you carry the Cross willingly, it will carry you. It will lead you to the place where suffering comes to an end, a place we will not find here. If you are forced against your will to carry the Cross, then you make it difficult for yourself, adding to your load. No matter what attitude you have, you must bear the burden. If you manage to throw away one cross, you will certainly find another, and it may be even heavier.

Do you think you can escape what no one else can avoid? Which of the saints was exempt? Not even our Lord Jesus Christ was spared! "Was it not necessary for the Messiah to suffer these things and then to enter his glory?" (Luke 24:26). How can you think you will find a way other than this royal highway of the holy Cross?

The whole life of Christ was a Cross and a martyrdom; do you want ease and recreation for yourself? You are making a grave mistake, and deceiving yourself, if you seek anything other than hardship. This mortal life is full of misery and it is marked on every side with crosses. The higher you advance in the Spirit, the heavier the crosses become, for the pain of exile increases in proportion to your love for God. And yet, a person afflicted in many ways still receives refreshing comfort if he sees the value of enduring crosses.

We are not naturally inclined

> to bear the Cross,
> to love the Cross,
> to discipline our bodies,
> to run away from honors,
> to suffer reproach willingly,
> to disregard ourselves and to wish to be disregarded,
> to endure all trouble and loss,
> to desire no prosperity in this world.

If you try to accomplish these things yourself, you will fail. But if you trust the Lord, you will receive divine strength, and you will be able to withstand the world and control your flesh.

Decide, then, like Christ's good and faithful servant, to bear courageously the Cross of your Lord, who, because of his love for you, was crucified. Drink heartily of the Lord's cup if you want to be his friend. As for comfort, leave that to God; let him do what he will. Accept suffering graciously. "I consider that what we suffer at this present time cannot be compared at all with the glory that is going to be revealed to us" (Rom. 8:18).

When you have reached such a point, all misery will seem sweet and you will relish it for Christ's sake and think that you have discovered paradise on earth.

As long as you object to suffering you will be ill at ease. Accept it, and you will find peace.

Even if you were caught up in the ecstasy of the third heaven with Paul, you would still face adversity. "I myself [says Christ] will show him all that he must suffer for my sake" (Acts 9:16). Therefore, you must suffer if you desire to love Jesus and to serve him always. If only you were worthy to suffer something for the name of Jesus! How much glory would be yours; what joy all God's saints would feel; how much you would teach your neighbor! For everyone advises patience, but few are willing to suffer.

Without doubt, you ought to lead a dying life. The more you die to yourself here, the more you begin to live for God. You are unprepared to comprehend heavenly things until you can submit to adversities for Christ's sake. Nothing is more acceptable to God, nothing more wholesome for you, than to suffer cheerfully for Christ. And if you have a choice, take the hard road. This will make you more like Christ.

You can be sure that if there had been a better way to man's salvation than suffering, Christ would have followed it. He plainly taught the bearing of the Cross. "If anyone wants to come with me, he must forget himself, take up his cross every day, and follow me" (Luke 9:23).

When we have read and searched through everything, this will be our ultimate conclusion: "We must pass through many troubles to enter the kingdom of God" (Acts 14:22).

PART III

CONVERSATIONS WITH GOD

Christ
Speaks Inwardly
to the
Faithful Soul

I will listen to what the Lord God says in me. That soul is blessed who hears the Lord speaking and inwardly receives his words of comfort.

Blessed are the ears that hear the divine whisper and ignore the murmuring of the world.

Truly blessed are the ears which listen to no external voice, but to the truth that is taught within.

Blessed are the eyes that are closed, focusing inwardly on eternal things.

Blessed are the ones who can enter deeply within

themselves; who prepare themselves more and more, by daily exercises, to receive heavenly secrets.

Blessed are those who take time for God, who shake off all the encumbering cares of the world.

Think about these things, O my soul, and close the door on your physical senses, that you may hear what God says within you.

Thus says your Beloved: 'I am your salvation, your peace, your life. Stay with me, and you shall find peace. Release everything that is transitory. Let it pass away. Look for lasting things. Short-term pleasures are seductive, but they will disappoint you. What good is everything in all creation to you if you are not in close fellowship with the Creator? Therefore, get rid of all earthly things.

Try to please your Maker. Be faithful to me. That way you will discover true happiness.'

The Truth Speaks Within Us Without Noisy Words

Speak, Lord, your servant is listening. I am your servant; help me to know and understand what you are saying. Let your teaching distill like dew.

Long ago, the Hebrews said to Moses, "If you speak to us, we will listen; but we are afraid that if God speaks to us, we will die" (Exod. 20:19).

But Lord, that is not what I pray. Instead, in all humility, I earnestly say with Samuel, "Speak, Lord, your servant is listening."

I am not listening now to Moses or any other prophet. I am listening for *you*, O God, the one who inspired and enlightened all the prophets. You alone can instruct me perfectly, and they can teach me nothing without you.

The prophets may speak words, but they cannot give the Spirit.

Their language is beautiful, but if you are silent, it will not set my heart on fire.

They give the words, but you give the words meaning.

They present mysteries, but you unlock what is hidden.

They announce commandments, but you help me keep them.

They show the way, but you give me strength to walk in it.

They reach my outward senses, but you enlighten me inwardly.

They water the garden, but you make the plants grow.

They cry out with words, but you help me understand.

Therefore, O Lord, speak your eternal truth to me through their words, so my life will not remain unfruitful. Then you will not condemn me for having heard without responding, for having known without loving, for having believed without obeying.

Speak, Lord, your servant is listening. You have the words of eternal life. Speak to me. Comfort my soul. Transform my life. I will give praise, glory, and honor to you always.

God
Is to Be
Heard with
Humility

Hear my words, my child—wholesome words that surpass all the knowledge of the philosophers and sages. My words are spirit and life and can never be compared with the wisdom of the world. They are not to be misused for self-satisfaction, but to be heard in silence, and received with humility and great affection.

"Lord, how happy is the person you instruct,
The one to whom you teach your law!
You give him rest from days of trouble" (Ps. 94:12-13).

I am the one who taught the prophets from the beginning. Even now I continue to speak to everyone, but many are spiritually deaf and do not hear my voice. Most people listen more eagerly to the world than to me. The world promises fleeting things of little value and people strive for them. I offer things of highest quality which endure forever, and people yawn in apathy.

Is there anyone who serves me with the same care and devotion given to the world and its leaders? To gain a few dollars, a long trip may be taken; for eternal life, many will barely lift a foot from the ground.

Blush with shame! You do not care at all for

permanent good, for the reward beyond all price, for the highest honor and glory that will last forever. Be ashamed, you lazy and complaining servant! You are more anxious to work for death than for life.

Those who seek earthly rewards will be disappointed frequently, but my promises deceive no one. I will not send anyone away empty if he trusts me. I will give what I promise. I will do what I say. I only require that a person remain faithful in my love.

Write my words in your heart; diligently meditate upon them. You will see how important they are to you when you are tempted. Even if you can't understand the meaning now, keep reading. A time will come when you will need those words and then you will understand.

I visit my friends in two ways:
1. with trials and temptations;
2. with consolation.

And I teach two lessons as the days go by:
1. Get rid of your vices.
2. Increase your virtues.

"Whoever rejects me and does not accept my message has one who will judge him. The words I have spoken will be his judge on the last day!" (John 12:48).

A Prayer
for the Grace
of Devotion

O Lord, my God! You are everything that is good. Who am I, that I should dare to speak to you? I am your poorest, least deserving servant—lowlier than I would like to admit.

Yet remember me, O Lord, because
    I am nothing,
    and I can do nothing.
Only you are good, just, and holy.
    You can do all things.
    You can supply all things.
    You fill all things,
leaving empty only the person who lives apart from you.

In your mercy, fill my heart with grace. How can I endure this life without your strength and mercy?
    "Don't hide yourself from your servant;
    I am in great trouble—answer me now!
    Come to me and save me;
    rescue me from my enemies" (Ps. 69:17-18).
    "I lift up my hands to you in prayer;
    like dry ground my soul is thirsty for you . . .
    You are my God;
    teach me to do your will.
    Be good to me, and guide me on a safe path"
    (Ps. 143:6, 10).
Teach me to do your will, O Lord, teach me to

live worthily and humbly before you; for you are
my wisdom, you know me intimately; you knew
me before the world was made, and before I was
born in the world.

Our Honest
Humility
Before God

My child, live honestly before me, and always
look for me with a simple heart. This will defend
you from evil and set you free from deceivers and
unjust slanderers. If the truth sets you free, then
you will be really free, and you will pay no attention to the empty comments of others.

*That's true, Lord. Let it be for me as you say. I want
your Truth to teach me, guard me, and preserve me
until the end of my days. Let it free me from every evil,
and I will walk with you in liberty.*

The Truth speaks: I will teach you what is pleasing to me. Think about your sins with great dis-
pleasure and sadness. Never think highly of yourself because you have done some good things.

The fact is, you are a sinner. Many passions en-
tangle and enslave you. By yourself you will always be quickly defeated, quickly overcome, quick-

ly disturbed, quickly unnerved.

You have nothing to be proud of, and much that should shame you. You are far weaker than you can comprehend.

Therefore, do not let anything you do seem very important to you. Let nothing seem great, nothing precious or admirable, nothing sophisticated, nothing high, nothing really worth having, except that which is eternal.

Take pleasure, above all else, in the eternal Truth. Always be displeased with your own unworthiness. The thing to fear, the thing to blame and run away from, is your sin, which ought to bother you more than the loss of any material thing.

Some are not sincere. Curiosity and pride make them wish to know my secrets and understand God's profundity. All the while they neglect themselves and their own salvation.

Some have their devotion only in books, some in paintings, some in statues and carvings.

Some have me often enough on their lips, but they have little of me in their hearts.

Others, with insight and self-denial, seek the eternal at all times. They are reluctant to hear about earthly things and are upset by the demands of nature. These understand what the Spirit of Truth says to them: disregard the world, and long for heaven.

The Results
of Divine
Love

I bless you, heavenly Father, Father of my Lord Jesus Christ, because you take notice of a creature like me. Merciful Father and God of all comfort, I give you thanks.

Come then, Lord God, Holy One who loves me! When you come into my heart, everything in me will leap with joy!

"You are my hiding place;
you will save me from trouble.
I sing aloud of your salvation,
because you protect me" (Ps. 32:7).

Because I am still imperfect and weak in love, I need your strength and comfort. Visit me frequently and teach me with holy discipline.

Free me from evil passions, and heal my heart of excessive desires; that being inwardly healthy, I may be prepared to love, and filled with courage to endure and persevere.

Love is a great good that makes every heavy thing light. It is not burdened by the load it carries, and it sweetens the bitter. Jesus' noble love inspires us to do great things and to long for a more nearly perfect life. Love wants to live in the heights, and not to be grounded by base things.

Nothing is sweeter than love,
nothing stronger,

nothing wider,

nothing more pleasant,

nothing more satisfying in heaven or on earth.

Because you, my God, give birth to love, you are love's natural resting place.

The one in love rejoices in his freedom. He gives all for everything, because he is familiar with One who is supreme above all—the Source of all that is good. He concentrates not on the gifts, but on the Giver.

Love does not meet standard requirements; it goes beyond all measurements.

Love notices no burdens,

thinks nothing of its labors,

willingly does more than it is able,

pleads no excuse of impossibility;

believes it can accomplish anything.

And it can. It makes up for many shortcomings; it opens the door for many possibilities.

Anyone in love knows what I am talking about.

Enlarge your love in me, Lord. I desire to swim in a sea of your love. I want to be possessed by love so that I can rise above myself. Let me sing love's song. Let me follow you, my Beloved. Let me love you more than myself, and love myself only for you.

Love treads lightly. It is sincere, kind, pleasant, and delightful. It is strong, patient, faithful, careful, longsuffering, brave, and never selfish.

Toward you, Lord, love must be devout and thankful—trusting and hoping always, even when I do not taste your sweetness. For no one can live in love without some pain.

If I am not ready to suffer all things, and to accept your will, I am not worthy of the title *lover*.

A lover is willing to embrace the difficult and the bitter, for the sake of his Beloved.

How to Recognize a True Lover

Child, you are not yet a true lover.

Why, O Lord?

Because you give up when a little opposition comes your way. You are too eager for consolation. A genuine lover stands his ground when tempted. He does not yield to the Enemy. "And I am not saying this because I feel neglected, for I have learned to be satisfied with what I have" (Phil. 4:11).

A true lover looks less at the gift and more at the love of the giver. He regards the demonstration of affection as more important than the value of the gift, and prizes the one loved more than any present.

Therefore, all is not lost if you sometimes feel less devotion toward me than you would like. Even the affection you sometimes have is one of my gifts to you—something of a foretaste of heaven. Don't count on it too much, because it comes and goes. But do resist the tendency of your mind toward evil, and reject the suggestions of the Devil.

Be strong! It is not an illusion that sometimes you are ecstatically carried away and then you return to your familiar faults. It seems that you unwillingly tolerate this shift, and as long as it is unpleasant to you, and you resist it, you will be rewarded.

Remember that your old Enemy tries with every trick he has to frustrate your desire for good, and to divert your attention from worship. He suggests many evil thoughts, hoping to fatigue you and frighten you away from prayer and holy reading. He hates humble confession; if he could manage it, he would even talk you out of Holy Communion.

Don't listen to him! Ignore his deceitful traps. When he recommends anything evil, say to him:

"Get away from me, Satan! You are an obstacle in my way, because these thoughts of yours don't come from God" (Matt. 16:23).

"The Lord is my light and my salvation;
I will fear no one.
The Lord protects me from all danger;
I will never be afraid" (Ps. 27:1).

"Even if a whole army surrounds me,
I will not be afraid;
even if enemies attack me,
I will still trust God" (Ps. 27:3).

Fight like a good soldier. And if, because you are weak, you sometimes fall, get up again strengthened by the experience, trusting my abundant grace. Then guard yourself against complacency and pride. Be warned by the fall of the proud who rely upon their own strength. Always be humble.

The Privacy of Devotion

My child, it is best for you to be private with your devotion. Don't think highly of yourself or talk too much about it. Don't let the quality of your devotion be an obsession. It is better to think less of yourself, and to consider yourself unworthy of this grace.

Some incautious people ruin themselves by attempting to produce an ecstatic devotional experience by their own will. Because they neglect to consider their own weakness, they attempt more than is pleasing to me and quickly lose all. Those who try to build a safe nest for themselves in heaven become helpless and thereby learn not to fly with their own wings, but to trust mine.

Those who think they are intelligent seldom accept guidance. It is better to have a little good judgment with humility, than great knowledge about many things with self-conceit. It is better for you to have little than much of what may make you proud.

You are not wise if, in a moment of difficulty, you become despondent and lose your confidence in me. Those who are too secure in peacetime will be overly dejected in time of war.

When spiritual fervor has been ignited in you, meditate on how it will be when that light leaves you. And when this happens, remember that the light may return again and its loss may be profitable by my design.

Your value is not calculated by the number of visions you have, by your skill in the Scriptures, or by your position in relation to others.

You are most worthy if you are truly humble and full of divine love, and if you seek only My honor.

Standing in God's Presence

I will speak to you, Lord, even though I am nothing but dust and ashes.

If I begin to think highly of myself, you stand next to me, and my sins are obvious. I cannot deny them.

But if I am humble, and control my ego, and stop

being self-centered, and reduce myself to the dust which surely I am, your grace will be gentle with me, and your light will come into my heart. Then all my self-esteem, however small it might be, will vanish in the deep valley of my nothingness.

In that place you will hold a mirror before me and show me what I am, what I have been, and what I have become; for I am nothing, and I did not know it.

See what happens when I am left to myself! I am nothing but weakness. But the very instant you show me your love, I become strong and filled with new joy. How wonderful to be suddenly free from my own heavy weight. Instead of sinking downward I am lifted up into your embrace!

Your love guards me from danger and assists me in so many ways. It preserves me from innumerable evils.

It is true, "Whoever loves his own life will lose it; whoever hates his own life in this world will keep it for life eternal" (John 12:25). By loving myself, I lose myself. But by looking only for you, and loving only you, I find both myself and you.

Blessed are you, my God. Even though I am unworthy, your generosity and goodness never cease. "For he makes his sun to shine on bad and good people alike, and gives rain to those who do good and to those who do evil" (Matt. 5:45).

Turn us in your direction, that we may be grateful, humble, and devout. You are our salvation, our courage, and our strength.

Putting
God
First

My child, I must be your life's supreme goal if you want genuine happiness. This will purify your intentions and keep you from perverse interest in yourself and earthly things. For if you put yourself first, you will begin to dry up and wither inside.

Give me first place, for I have given all. Think about how everything flows from the Greatest Good. I am the source, like a spring that produces a river. From my resources the small and the great, the poor and the rich, fill themselves, as from an inexhaustible fountain, with the water of life.

Those who willingly and freely serve me shall receive "one blessing after another" (John 1:16). But those who attempt to delight in anything other than me, or to enjoy some private pleasure, will not have true joy and will get into innumerable difficulties.

Therefore, don't take credit for anything good yourself, and don't attribute goodness to any other person. Give me the praise; for without me no one amounts to anything.

I have given you everything you have and I want you to be grateful. This will check pride. And if you are filled with heavenly grace and genuine love, you will not be envious or narrowminded, and selfishness will be impossible for you. For di-

vine love is stronger than all else and it enlarges the
capacity of the soul.

If you are thinking clearly, you will rejoice in me
alone and place all of your hope in me, for "there is
only One who is good" (Matt. 19:17). I am to be
praised above all things.

Serving
God at
Any Cost

Now I will speak again, O Lord. I will express
myself in the presence of my Lord and my heavenly King.

> "How wonderful are the good things
> you keep for those who honor you!
> Everyone knows how good you are,
> how securely you protect those who trust you"
> (Ps. 31:19).

What difference do you make to those who love
you and serve you with enthusiasm? You allow
them the indescribable joy of contemplating you.

You have given me a special insight into the
sweetness of your love: you gave me my life; when
I wandered far away, you brought me back again
to serve you; you wanted me to love you.

You are a waterfall of unceasing love! What shall I say about you? How can I forget you? You thought of me even when I was lost and desperate. You have been merciful beyond my wildest dream. You have been good to me far above anything I deserve.

How shall I pay you back? Most of us are not expected to give up everything, to renounce the world and begin a life of monastic solitude. Does it mean very much that I should serve you when all of creation exists for that purpose? I don't think so. But I see this, and it staggers me: you are willing to accept the service of someone as poor and unworthy as I. You will make me one of your beloved servants.

I am your servant! Everything I have is yours. But even as I say that, I know you are serving me more than I am serving you. At your command all of the resources of heaven and earth are at my disposal, and even the angels help me. Yet you serve me in a way that surpasses all of this: you promise to give yourself to me. You are the great Servant of us all.

With what gift can I return your favors? I want to serve you all the days of my life. I wish it were possible, just for one day, to do something worthwhile for you. You are my Lord, and I am a poor servant who is obligated to serve you with all my strength. I should never tire of praising you, for this is what I want to do. This is my desire. Compensate for what I lack.

Examine and
Control
Your Desires

My child, there are still many things you need to learn.

What are they, Lord?

That you desire only what will please me, and that you stop putting yourself first and earnestly seek my will.

Sometimes you are driven to distraction by desires which burn inside you. But try to determine whether your underlying motive is to honor me or simply to serve your own best interests. If you seek to honor me, you will find contentment whatever happens, but if selfishness hides within you, it will become your greatest burden. Be careful, therefore, not to give in too easily to any desire without seeking my counsel.

Sometimes apparently good things are not desirable, and what is offensive at first sight often turns out to be the better choice.

It can be worthwhile to restrain even the best desires and inclinations. Excessive eagerness distracts the mind, a lack of discipline can lead to scandal, and, if others resist your wishes, the disappointment may turn you away from me.

Your sensual appetite may require extreme measures to control. It is not easy to disregard what your flesh likes and dislikes, and to train an unwilling body to be subject to the Spirit. You must work at this, and, eventually, your body will obey you. You will learn to be content with little, to be pleased with simple things, and not to complain about inconveniences.

Patience Wins Over Sensual Desires

O *Lord, my God, I know that patience is necessary for me because many things disturb me every day. No matter what plans I make to keep myself at peace, I cannot avoid life's struggle and sorrow*

That is true, my child. I do not desire for you to enjoy an absolute peace, free from all temptations and hindrances. Instead, I want you to have peace even when you are troubled by unpleasant experiences.

Do you believe that prosperous people have an easy life? Ask them and you will find out otherwise. You may think they are carefree, and do not bleed like regular people. But, even if all that nonsense is true at this moment, how long do you think it will last? "As smoke is blown away, so he drives them off" (Ps. 68:2). The time always comes when former pleasures can barely be recalled. These "privileged" people live with constant bitterness, weariness, and fear. The very things they enjoy so much often bring them sorrow. Such brief pleasures are false pleasures, but few can see this. Many forfeit their souls for small enjoyments in this corruptible life.

Therefore, "Don't be controlled by your lust; keep your passions in check" (Sirach 18:30). "Seek your happiness in the Lord, and he will give you your heart's desire" (Ps. 37:4).

For you will only truly enjoy your life and receive my full comfort if you stop those practices which debase you. The less you depend upon earthly comfort, the sweeter you will find my consolation.

You will have some sadness when you begin this battle in yourself. Old habits will resist you, but you will win if you replace them with better habits. Your body will protest, but your spirit can gain the upper hand. The old serpent will tempt and harass you, but prayer will make him run away. And the best way to keep him away is to get busy with something constructive.

Following Christ's Example of Humble Obedience

My child, if you try to escape obedient service, you will miss my gift. A community has benefits which are unknown to the hermit.

If you are unable to freely and cheerfully submit to a superior, it is a sign that you do not have yourself under control. Learn how to submit quickly to a leader if you want to rule yourself. It is easier to defeat the outward enemy if the inward man is strong and controlled. The most troublesome enemy you have is yourself, if you are not in harmony with my Spirit.

It is an indication that you still love yourself too much if you are afraid to submit to others. What a paltry comparison if you, nothing but dust and ashes, submit yourself to others in the Lord, when I, the Almighty and most high God, the Creator of everything, subjected myself to the world for your sake! I became the most humble and submissive of all people, that you might overcome your pride with my humility.* Discover how to break your own wishes and to give in to the will of others. Be firm with yourself and don't let pride swell your chest. Find out what it is like to let someone walk over you if necessary.

What do you have to complain about? If you

were to receive what you have earned, you would be condemned to hell. But I have spared you because you are precious to me. I want you to know my love.

———————————

*The original author passed up a splendid opportunity to quote the great passage recorded in Philippians 2:6-11.
"He always had the nature of God,
but he did not think that by force he should try
to become equal with God.
Instead of this, of his own free will he gave up all he had,
and took the nature of a servant.
He became like man
and appeared in human likeness.
He was humble and walked the path of obedience
all the way to death—his death on the cross."

God Is Not
Misled
by a Few
Good Deeds

———————————

Lord, I tremble before your thundering judgment. It astonishes me when I read:
"Can any man be really pure?
Can anyone be right with God?
Why, God does not trust even his angels;
even they are not pure in his sight"
(Job 15:14-15).

If angels are faulty, what can I say for myself? If stars even fall from heaven, what can I expect? I have seen good and great people stumble, and those who have eaten sacred bread now root with pigs.

The only good thing about me is what you give. The only clear thoughts I have are a gift from you. I have no strength unless you uphold me, no morality unless you protect me. Leave me on my own, and I sink into death; guide me, and I am raised up to life.

How could I ever boast? Your judgment destroys my self-righteousness. No one in the whole world can sit at the head table when he has faced the Truth.

How to
Pray for
the Things
We Want

My child, this is the way to pray: "Lord, if it is pleasing to you, fulfill my request. If this will honor you, let it be done in your name. If it is good for me, grant that I may use it for your honor. But if you know that it will hurt me, take the desire away from me. "

Why pray like that? Because not every desire is inspired by the Holy Spirit, even though it may seem right and good. Sometimes it is hard to tell whether a notion is an inspiration or a temptation. Many have been deceived.

Therefore, every request must be made with humility. You must submit the entire matter to me, take yourself entirely out of it, and say: "O Lord, you know what is best. Let this or that be done as you please. Give what you choose, how much you choose, and when you choose. Place me where you think best and treat me as you see fit. I am in your hand. Turn me in one direction and then another; I am your servant, prepared for anything. I have no desire to live for myself, but only for you. How I wish I could do this perfectly!"

Trusting God

Friend, let me do what is best for you. You see everything from a human point of view

Lord, you are right. You care about me more than I care about myself. Unless I trust you, I have no ground to stand upon. Do with me whatever you choose, because it can only be good. If you want me to be in darkness, I will bless you; if you want me to be in light, I will bless you again. If I am comforted, I will be grateful; and if I am afflicted, I will be equally grateful.

My child, that is the way to think if you want to walk with me. Be as ready to suffer as to rejoice. Be as cheerful when poor as you would be when rich.

O Lord, for your sake I will gladly bear what I must, whatever it may be. I will accept good and evil, sweet and bitter, joy and sorrow, and for all of it I will give you thanks. As long as you stay close to me and never remove my name from the "book of the living" (Rev. 3:5), whatever trouble I experience will not hurt me.

How to Take Slights and Injuries

My child, I gave up the glories of heaven and accepted the miseries of this world because of my love for you, intending that you might learn a little patience. From the moment of my birth until my death on the Cross, I experienced grief. I was deprived of many things. I heard many complaints against me. I *calmly endured disgrace and taunting. For kindness I was repaid ingratitude. For miracles I received curses. When I spoke the truth, people argued with me.*

My Lord, since you were patient, I also should bear myself patiently. Although life can be bleak, it can become bright again with your help. If you had not lived before us to show the way, how could we follow? Even now we are only half-hearted. What would become of us if we did not have such great light?

Genuine Patience

What are you saying, my child? Stop complaining! Think about my sacrifice and the suffering of other saints. "For in your struggle against sin you have not yet had to resist to the point of being killed" (Heb. 12:4).

You have suffered very little in comparison with others. Think about the heavy burdens others carry, and you will easily bear your own small troubles. And if you do not think yours are small, perhaps it is only because you are impatient. Whether they are small or great, try to bear your burdens without complaint.

Do not say, "I can't take it! I'm not required to take it! This person has hurt me deeply and accused me of things that are not true." That is foolish. It fails to take the crowning virtue of patience into account; it focuses on the offending person and the injury.

You are not patient if you are willing to accept difficulty only up to a certain point and from a few selected people. Genuine patience cares nothing about the source of the problem, whether it is from a superior, an equal, or an inferior; whether it is from a good and holy person or a villain. You must take it all thankfully, as though I gave it. Consider it your gain. For it is impossible that anything, however small, can be suffered for my sake without some reward.

Be ready for battle if you want to win. Without struggling you cannot gain patience, and if you will not suffer, you refuse to be crowned. Rest only follows labor.

Lord, let this become possible for me, even though it seems out of reach. You know I can endure so very little and I am quickly defeated. Please let every difficulty become a desirable thing, for to suffer and to be harassed for you is beneficial to my soul.

Admitting
Our
Weakness

I will confess my weakness to you, O Lord. Sometimes when I intend to be courageous, I succumb even to a little temptation.

You know how frail I am, Lord. Have mercy on me. Do not let me get stuck in a quagmire of sin. I fall so easily. My passions are stronger than my will, and, although I am reluctant, they keep on nagging me. It is fatiguing to live every day in that kind of tension. I know I am weak, because temptations come to me far more easily than they depart.

What a strange life! Trouble and misery are always in stock. Traps and enemies are abundant. When one problem retreats, another takes its place. And sometimes the second difficulty doesn't wait for the first to be resolved.

How can anyone love a life like that? Isn't it natural to feel bitterness in the face of so much misery? Is anything so threatened by death and plague even worthy of the name, "life"? And yet people love it and try to find happiness in it. Some things make us love this world; other things make us hate it.

Complete
Devotion
to God

Above all else, and in everything, my soul must rest in God. Let me, O living Jesus, rest in you above every created thing,

 above health and beauty,
 above glory and honor,
 above power and dignity,
 above wisdom and cunning,
 above riches and arts,
 above joy and gladness,
 above fame and praise,
 above pleasure and comfort,
 above hope and promise,
 above things earned and things desired,
 above gifts and favors,
 above mirth and merrymaking.

Ultimately let me rest above angels and archangels and all the host of heaven, above things seen and unseen, above all that is not you, my God.

 Because you, O Lord, are above all. You alone are most high,

 most powerful,
 most sufficient,
 most full,
 most pleasant,
 most comforting.

No matter what gifts you give me, and regardless of your great self-revelation, if I do not know you as my closest friend, I am still hungry for you. I will never be content until my heart is devoted above all else to you.*

When will this happen? When will I love you so much, my God, that I forget myself and know you alone?

Now, I sigh unhappily. I am hurt and grieved by the evil I see. I am hindered and distracted, allured and entangled, and the way to you is cut off like a drawbridge pulled up.

Let my sighs be prayers.

How long will you wait, Lord? When will you come to help me? Please come help me. Without you I cannot enjoy a single day or even an hour. You are my joy; apart from you I sit at an empty table. I am wretched, like a prisoner in chains. Let the sun shine on me again. Give me freedom and liberty. Smile at me, Lord.

Others can chase after what they will, but I want only you. I will pray, and keep on praying, until your kind favor returns and I hear you speaking to me inwardly once again.

I am here, my friend. You have called, and I have come. Your tears and the longing of your soul, your humility and repentance, have brought me to you.

Lord, I have called you and desired you. I am willing to make any sacrifice for you. It was you who gave me this thirst for you, you who stirred the ashes and fanned the flame of my desire for you.

What more can I say to you now? I bow in

humility, confess my sin, and praise your greatness.

_____

*This is a reference to the famous line near the beginning of St. Augustine's *Confessions*: "Thou madest us for Thyself, and our heart is restless, until it repose in Thee."

The Distribution of God's Favors

_____

You are the giver of all we have and are, O God.

If one has received more, and another less, both are yours, and without you there is no blessing at all.

The one who has received the most cannot say that he deserved it or think that he is any better than others. The greatest and the best, after all, is the one who thinks the least of himself and is humbly grateful.

If someone has received less, he must not be disturbed about it. And certainly he shouldn't envy anyone else. Instead he should turn to you, Lord, and praise you for your goodness and your gifts.

You know what is suitable for everyone. You have a reason for giving one less and another more.

This is not for us to figure out.

Those who have received less can take special comfort because, "God purposely chose what the world considers nonsense in order to shame the wise, and he chose what the world considers weak in order to shame the powerful. He chose what the world looks down on and despises, and thinks is nothing, in order to destroy what the world thinks is important (1 Cor. 1:27-28).

Four Things That Bring Peace

*M*y child, now I will teach you the way of peace and true freedom.

Lord, I am eager to hear.

1. *Do what pleases another rather than yourself.*
2. *Choose to have less rather than more.*
3. *Seek the lowest place and be the servant of all.*
4. *Pray that my will may be accomplished in you always.*

Do these four things, and you will surely find peace and inward rest.

My Lord, this short lesson is perfect. With a few words you have struck the target with great force. I can repeat the lesson in a moment, but its truth is gigantic.

Now, if I could simply follow it, I would not be troubled so easily. For whenever I am upset and burdened, it is because I have not practiced these simple rules. I cannot attain it on my own, but you can do all things. Help me.

A Prayer Against Evil Thoughts

Don't stay so far away, O God;
   my God, hurry to my aid!" (Ps. 71:12).
   I have evil thoughts, and I am afraid. How can I destroy them? How can I survive without being hurt?

This is your answer to me:
   "I myself will prepare your way,
   leveling mountains and hills.
   I will break down bronze gates
   and smash their iron bars.
   I will give you treasures from dark, secret places;
   then you will know that I am the Lord" (Isa. 45:2-3).

Do as you say, O Lord. Let every evil thought fly away from your holy presence.

A Prayer
for the
Clearing
of My Mind

Clear my thinking, Lord Jesus, with the light you shine within me. Chase all darkness from my mind. Check my wandering thoughts and fight for me. Enter into combat with these ugly beasts (my body's appetites), so there may be "peace inside your walls and safety in your palaces" (Ps. 122:7).

Command the stormy winds to cease; order the waves to be still. Create a great calm in me.

"Send your light and your truth;
may they lead me . . ." (Ps. 43:3).

For I am "formless and desolate" (Gen. 1:2), until you enlighten me. Lift up my mind. Make me so much at home with heavenly things that it will annoy me even to think of earthly things.

Staying Out
of Others'
Business

Child, there are some things not worth thinking about. "What is that to you? Follow me!" (John 21:22).

For what difference does it make to you what someone else becomes, or says, or does? You do not need to answer for others, only for yourself. Why get mixed up in such things? I know everyone and see everything that is done under the sun. I understand the dynamics of every situation, and I know each person's thoughts, attitudes, and intentions. All of this is my business, not yours. Don't worry about it. I am not deceived.

False Peace
and True Peace

Peace is what I leave with you; it is my own peace that I give you. I do not give it as the world does. Do not be worried and upset; do not be afraid" (John 14:27).

Everyone wants peace, but very few care for the things that produce it. My peace is with the humble and gentle, and especially with the patient. If you will listen to me, and act accordingly, you will enjoy much peace.

What shall I do, Lord?

Pay attention to what you do and say. Care for nothing other than pleasing me. Do not judge others or meddle in things which do not concern you. Following this advice will spare you needless trouble. But remember that it is impossible to be entirely free of trouble and fatigue in this life.

Don't think that you have found true peace just because you feel no pain or have no enemies. Never think that life is perfect when you receive everything you want, and never consider yourself my favorite child because you enjoy a great devotional life. That is not the way to true peace and spiritual growth.

What is the way, Lord?

It is in offering your whole heart to me, forgetting your own will in great things and small things, thanking me equally for the pleasant and the unpleasant, weighing all these things in the same balance.

And if you are strong enough to willingly suffer more and more without praising yourself but always praising my name, then you will be on the road to true peace and you will have the hope of seeing me in the everlasting joy of heaven.

Take Necessities
in Moderation

Food, drink, clothing, and all things necessary for staying alive are a burden to a fervent spirit. Let me use such things in moderation, and never prize them too much. I must not renounce them entirely, because you want us to support nature. But to ask for more than enough, and for great pleasures, would be wrong. Guide me and teach me so that I will know when I have had enough.

The Greatest
Barrier:
Self-love

Give everything to everyone; withhold none of your love. Nothing injures you more than self-love.

Desire nothing illegal.

Own nothing that will enslave you.

Why weary yourself with extra cares? Accept my will and you will lose nothing.

If you constantly search for the perfect experience or the perfect location to improve your life, you will never be satisfied or free from anxiety. In every situation something will be missing, and in every place someone will cross you.

Happiness, then, is not found by increasing your possessions, but by despising them. Renounce your craving not only for wealth, but also for prestige and fame. All of these will pass away with this world.

Your place doesn't matter; your spirit does. You can change jobs and locations without changing yourself for the better, if your heart has no foundation in me. For you will always find again, in the new place, the very thing you were running away from—sometimes more of it!

Accepting Slander

Child, do not be destroyed if some people don't like you and say unfair things about you. If your soul is well-ordered, you won't pay much attention to flying words.

It is great wisdom to keep silent when damaging words are spoken to you. Turn your attention to me and don't worry about rumor and slander.

Don't look for support from the mouths of others. You are who you are regardless of what they say. And you shall know much peace if you neither try to please them, nor care if you displease them.

Call on God When You Need Him

I am in an inescapable difficulty, Lord, and I turn to you for help. Use this bad moment for some good purpose.

"Now my heart is troubled—and what shall I say? Shall I say, 'Father, do not let this hour come upon me'? But that is why I came—so that I might go through this hour of suffering. Father, bring glory to your name!" (John 12:27-28). "Save me, Lord! Help me now!" (Ps. 40:13). For what can I do to help myself? Where can I go without you? Give me patience in this emergency. Help me, my God, and I will not be afraid.

In the middle of this adversity, what shall I say? "Your will be done" (Matt. 6:10). It is not surprising that I suffer, and I ought to bear it. Yes, I want to bear it patiently, until the storm is over and a better time comes. You are able to take even this trouble away from me. You can soften its impact, as you have before, so I will not collapse under it. The more difficult the problem is for me, the easier it is for you to solve.

Recovery

My child, I am the Lord who "protects his people in times of trouble" (Nah. 1:7). Come to me whenever you have a problem. I could help you much faster if you were not so slow in turning to prayer, but you try everything else first. Remember that I am the one who rescues those who trust in me. You will find no lasting help in any other source.

Now that you have caught your breath and your trouble has passed, recuperate in my mercies. I stand near you to repair all damage and to make things better than before. Is anything too hard for me? Where is your faith? Stand strong in me. Have patience and courage; comfort will come in time. Wait. I will come to you with healing.

Are you anxious about the future? What will that gain you but sorrow? "So do not worry about tomorrow; it will have enough worries of its own. There is no need to add to the troubles each day brings" (Matt. 6:34).

What a waste to be disturbed or joyful about future events which may never materialize! The Enemy will prey on your natural inclination to such anxieties. He doesn't care whether he deludes you to love the present or to fear the future.

"Do not be worried and upset; do not be afraid" (John 14:27). When you think you are far from me, I am frequently quite near. When you feel that all is lost, sometimes the greatest gain is ready to be yours. Don't judge everything by the way you feel right now. If, for a while, you feel no comfort from me, I have not rejected you. In fact, I have set you on the road to the kingdom of heaven.

It is better for you to experience a little adversity than to have everything exactly as you choose. Otherwise, you may become mistakenly self-satisfied. What I have given, I can take away, and I can return it again when I please. When I give something to you, it is on loan; when I take it back, I am not asking for anything that is yours. "Every good gift and every perfect present comes from heaven; it comes down from God" (James 1:17).

"I love you just as the Father loves me; remain in my love" (John 15:9). That is what I said to my beloved disciples, and you will notice that I sent them out into the world,

> not to enjoy earthly pleasures, but to do battle;
> not to receive honor, but to receive contempt;
> not to be idle, but to work;

> not to rest, but to reap a harvest patiently.

Remember these words, my child.

Forget
Created Things
and Find
the Creator

Lord, I lack the spiritual maturity to live so that nothing in creation, none of life's pleasures or irritations, can hinder my devotion to you. I know how the psalmist felt when he sang,

"I wish I had wings, like a dove.

I would fly away and find rest" (Ps. 55:6).

Who is more at rest than the one who cares for no earthly thing? For you, the Creator of all things, have made no creature that compares with you. And, unless I can be liberated from a love of created things, my mind will not be free to concentrate on you alone. This explains why so few of us are contemplative people. Most of us find the requirements too great. We need your grace.

What is not God is nothing. And that is the label we ought to put on it: "Nothing!"

Self-denial

My child, the only way to possess absolute freedom is to renounce yourself. Those who seek their own interests are trapped. They love themselves. They wander around in circles greedily searching for soft and delicate things instead of the things of Christ. They make plans that are doomed to fail because they are not in harmony with me.

Here is my teaching again in a capsule: Let everything go, and you will find everything; stop wanting so much, and you will have rest.

Lord, this is not going to be easy. You're asking for perfection!

Don't be frightened off, my child. Gain an appetite for higher things. I have no greater wish for you than this: that you lose all your selfishness and serve only me. Yes, you have a long way to go. But unless you start the journey, you will never reach the end.

"I advise you, then, to buy gold from me, pure gold, in order to be rich" (Rev. 3:18). That gold is heavenly wisdom which sees every worldly thing as contemptible garbage. This treasure remains hidden from many.

Swinging
Moods

_____

So you feel one way today! You will feel another way tomorrow. Like it or not, you will be somewhat manic-depressive as long as you live:

> Some days you'll be happy and other days you'll be sad,
>> some days calm and other days troubled,
>> some days faithful and other days faithless,
>> some days vigorous and other days sluggish,
>> some days solemn and other days lighthearted.

But if you are well-taught by the Spirit, you will live above such changes. You will pass through your various moods unshaken and push on toward your goal of seeking me only.

The clearer your target, the better you will weather emotional storms.

Delight
in God

I love you, my God. You are all I could ask for. What more can I desire? When you are present, I live in delight. You give me a calm heart, a tranquil mind, and a festive spirit. With your help I can rejoice in all circumstances and praise you at all times.

Nothing is tasteless to those who hunger for you. But nothing can satisfy those who refuse to taste you.

You are the everlasting Light, outshining all created lights. Send your bright beams to penetrate me. Purify and illuminate me with their great power. Give me new life.

Everyone
Is Tempted

My child, you will never be free from temptation in this life. You will always need spiritual armor, for you live among enemies who attack at every opportunity. If you don't shield yourself, you will not escape without injury. And if you fail to abandon everything else for me, you will not be equal to the task. Be brave! Winning will be worth the fight, but losing will bring misery and pain.

If you look for rest now, how will you attain heavenly rest? Don't ask for rest; ask for patience.

Be glad to endure everything because of your love for me:

labor,
pain,
temptation,
nuisance,
anxiety,
compulsion,
sickness,
injury,
slander,
reprimand,
humiliation,
confusion,
correction,
and contempt.

These are distressing trials for a new Christian, but they will make you a better person and prepare you for something magnificent. For a brief effort, you will receive an everlasting reward, and for a passing difficulty, infinite glory.

Will you always enjoy spiritual comfort? No, even my most devoted saints had problems, temptations, and feelings of desolation. But they endured it all patiently, trusting me rather than themselves, knowing that the suffering of "this present time cannot be compared at all with the glory that is going to be revealed" (Rom. 8:18). It is ridiculous for you to expect to receive instantly what others have barely obtained after many tears and great spiritual fatigue.

Wait patiently for me. Control your behavior. Take courage and never stop serving me because of suffering or fear. Offer your very life for my glory. I will reward you for it, and I will not desert you when you are in trouble.

God and Your Business

Give your business to me, my child, and I will make it prosper as I see fit. Wait for me to take care of it and you will be glad.

O Lord, I gladly give it all to you because my efforts accomplish so little. I wish I did not care so much about success.

My child, sometimes a person grasps and claws for something, but when he obtains it, he finds that some other goal is more desirable. A person's interests often change. True and lasting profit comes only from self-denial, for the one who denies himself lives in freedom and security.

Pride
Cannot Be
Justified

When I look at the sky, which you have made,

at the moon and the stars, which you set in their places—

what is man, that you think of him;

mere man, that you care for him?" (Ps. 8:3-4).

Have we deserved any favors, Lord? What right do I have to complain if you neglect me completely? If you don't give me what I want, what just reason do I have to grumble?

Lord, I am nothing,

I can do nothing,

I possess nothing in myself that is worthwhile,

I am distressingly insufficient,

and give all my attention to trivia.

Unless you help me, there is no hope for me.

Any praise belongs to you, not to me. In you I will rejoice, but as for me, "I will not boast about myself, except the things that show how weak I am" (2 Cor. 12:5).

Being
Honored Is
Unimportant

---

*M**y child, do not let it bother you if you see others getting recognition and honors while you are overlooked. Turn to me and the neglect of people will not trouble you.*

Lord, we are blind and insanely vain. Unless I am willing to be totally unrecognized, I will never find any peace within me, or become spiritually enlightened, or be at one with you.

God Is
the Best
Teacher

D**o not be led astray by the brightest human minds. "For the Kingdom of God is not a matter of words but of power" (1 Cor. 4:20).

Never read anything in order to appear wise. Knowing answers to difficult questions will not help you nearly as much as spiritual discipline. Even after profound scholarship, you still need to know me, for I am the Beginning of everything, "the teacher of all men" (Ps. 94:10). I will give you better insight than any professor could. I teach without audible words, and without argument and debate. I instruct you to despise earthly things and seek the eternal, to run from honors and endure insults, to place all hope in me and to love me above all things.

Books may contain identical letters and use the same method of communication, but they do not instruct everyone in the same way. The reason is that I secretly teach within each person as I see fit.

A Word of Divine Encouragement

My child, do not be worn out by the work you are doing for me. Let no setback discourage you. I will give you strength.

Remember, you will not be working here forever. If you will wait a little while, things will change. Soon enough all labor and trouble will end.

Keep going, then. Work faithfully in my garden, and I will be your wages. Write, read, sing, mourn, be silent, and pray. Take all blows gladly. The kingdom of heaven is worth all this and much more. When you know the joy of that peace, you will no longer ask, "Who will rescue me from this body that is taking me to death?" (Rom. 7:24), for death will be destroyed and you will remain with me forever.

A Prayer for Troubled Times

Heavenly Father, the time has come for me to be tested. It is proper that I should now suffer something for your sake. Before time began you knew this hour would come. Outwardly, I will be tormented; inwardly, I will be with you. For a little while, I will be a failure and an object of scorn. Go down with me Father, so I may rise with you in the dawning of a new light.

Such humbling is good for me, Lord. It helps me throw away haughtiness and pride. It is valuable "that I am covered with shame" (Ps. 69:7), because it makes me turn to you for comfort rather than to men. Thank you for this painful challenge. You know how troubled times can scour away the rust of sin. Do with me as you choose.

O Lord,
let me know what is worth knowing,
love what is worth loving,
praise what pleases you,
honor what is worthy in your sight,
and avoid all that is evil.

As humble Saint Francis said, "A man is as much as he is in your sight, and no more."

Enduring the Desert

My child, you cannot always be spiritually high and inflamed with devotion. You are flesh and bones, and naturally inclined to stumble. As long as you live in a mortal body, you will face weariness.

Bear patiently your exile and the dryness of your mind. The time will come when I will make you forget these painful moments and you will enjoy inward quietness. I will open the Bible for you and you will be thrilled by your new understanding of my truth. Then you will say, "I consider that what we suffer at this present time cannot be compared at all with the glory that is going to be revealed to us" (Rom. 8:18).

A Prayer
for Grace

My Lord, give me the grace which you have showed me is so important for my spiritual health. Let me overcome my natural inclinations. I can't resist these passions unless you help me. "I know that good does not live in me—that is, in my human nature. For even though the desire to do good is in me, I am not able to do it. I don't do the good I want to do; instead, I do the evil that I do not want to do" (Rom. 7:18-19). So it is that I start many good things, but then drop out before the job is finished.

Therefore, O Lord, let your grace lead me and follow me, through your son, Jesus Christ. Amen.

Following
Christ

My child, the more you can withdraw from yourself, the more you can enter into me. I want you to learn how to forget yourself completely and be comfortable in my will. Follow me. "I am the way, the truth, and the life" (John 14:6).

Without the Way, you can go nowhere.

Without the Truth, you can know nothing.

Without the Life, you cannot live.

I am the Way you should follow.

I am the Truth you should believe.

I am the Life you can hope for.

I am the Way that is protected.

I am the Truth that is flawless.

I am the Life that has no end.

I am the straightest Way.

I am the perfect Truth.

I am the happiest Life.

"If you obey my teaching . . . you will know the truth, and the truth will set you free" (John 8:31-32).

"Keep the commandments if you want to enter life" (Matt. 19:17).

If you want to know the truth, believe me.

"If you want to be perfect, go and sell all you have" (Matt. 19:21).

If you want to be my disciple, deny yourself everything. If you want a happy life, despise this present one.

If you want to be great in heaven, humble yourself in the world.

If you want to reign with me, bear the Cross with me.

Don't Question God's Judgment

My child, it will be better for you if you accept my decisions without complaint. Do not ask me to defend my actions, or to explain why one person is favored and another seems slighted. The answers to these questions go far beyond your comprehension.

When you are tempted to object, say with the psalmist, "You are righteous, Lord, and your laws are just" (Ps. 119:137). "The judgments of the Lord are just; they are always fair" (Ps. 19:9). My decisions are to be respected; they are not to be debated.

And don't waste your time trying to determine which of the saints is most saintly, or who shall be the greatest in the kingdom of heaven. This can cause arguments and dissension, and you may even form parties and admiration societies. The saints would be the first to tell you to stop it!

Some people gather around one godly person, and others gather around another. But this is human love, not divine love. I made all the saints. I gave them grace and glory. I chose them; they did not choose me. I attracted them to myself and led them safely through temptations. I gave them strength and patience.

But I do not reserve my favor for these saints; I

love everyone. So, if you look down on the least person, you fail to honor the greatest, because I made both of them and all in my kingdom are one, bound together in my love.

When the disciples asked who would be the greatest, this was Jesus' answer: "Unless you change and become like children, you will never enter the Kingdom of heaven. The greatest in the Kingdom of heaven is the one who humbles himself and becomes like this child" (Matt. 18:3-4).

The Prayer of One Who Would Follow Christ

I look only to you, merciful Father, for help and comfort. My soul praises you and seeks to become your holy dwelling place. Let nothing in me offend you. Hear the prayer of your weakest servant who is wandering in a distant place. Protect me from the dangers of this corruptible world. Guide me along the way of peace to my home of eternal brightness. Amen.

PART IV

PREPARATION FOR THE LORD'S SUPPER

Christ Invites
Us to His
Table

***

Christ the Beloved, Speaks:

"Come to me, all of you who are tired from carrying heavy loads, and I will give you rest" (Matt. 11:28). "I am the living bread that came down from heaven. If anyone eats this bread, he will live forever. The bread that I will give him is my flesh, which I give so that the world may live" (John 6:51). "Take and eat it; this is my body" (Matt. 26:26). "Do this in memory of me" (1 Cor. 11:24). "Whoever eats my flesh and drinks my blood lives in me, and I live in him. What gives life is God's Spirit; man's power is of no use at all. The words I have spoken to you bring God's life-giving Spirit" (John 6:56,63).

The Follower Speaks:

These are your words, Lord Jesus. You did not say them all at one time, and they are not written in one place, but they are your eternal Truth and I gratefully receive them in faith. They are your words; I claim them for myself. From your mouth they travel to my heart. They arouse me, for they are the tender words of love.

But I am afraid. My conscience hurts me and I squirm under the guilt of my sin.

Your words invite me to come confidently, but who am I, Lord, that I should dare approach you? How shall I even consider it when I know how unworthy I am? Angels and archangels bow in awe before you; holy and righteous people tremble before you, and yet I hear you say to me, "Come." Only because it is *your* command, can I believe it.

I am stunned. I am about to be the guest not of an angel, but of the Lord of angels! And in your presence I must have nothing in my heart and mind but you.

Then why don't I prepare myself more diligently to receive your sacred gifts? Why am I less eager than the patriarchs and prophets to enter your presence?

If the Lord's Supper were served in only one place, by only one ordained person in the world, many would make a sacred pilgrimage to experience it. But Communion celebrations are offered everywhere.

You come to me, Lord! You desire to be with me! Open my eyes that I might comprehend this mystery. Strengthen me with undoubting faith.

This Communion is health to my soul and body. It cures my vices, subdues my passions, lessens and defeats my temptations. It increases my virtues, confirms my faith, strengthens my hope, and ignites my love. And while I cannot yet be perfect, or as glowing as the cherubim and seraphim, I will prepare my heart to obtain some small flame of divine fire through this living sacrament.

The Beloved Speaks:

If you were as pure as an angel and as holy as John the Baptist, you still would not be worthy to touch this bread and wine. It is not because you deserve it that you should take Communion. Therefore, approach it with respect and reverence.

The Follower Speaks:

When I weigh your goodness on one side of a balance and my sinfulness on the other, I am shaken by what I see about myself. What shall I do, my God?

Teach me the right way. Show me some devotional exercise that will prepare me for the Holy Table. I want to prepare my heart.

The Beloved Speaks:

Examine your conscience. In humble confession and contrition it will be purified and cleared. You must bring no burden that will make you remorseful.

When you have done all you can with such a review, and when you sincerely regret your failures, and turn to me for forgiveness, you shall receive it. " 'If an evil man stops sinning and keeps my laws, if he does what is right and good, he will not die; he will certainly live. All his sins will be forgiven, and he will live, because he did what is right. Do you think I enjoy seeing an evil man die?' asks the sovereign Lord. 'No, I would rather see him repent and live' " (Ezek. 18:21–23).

The Follower Speaks:

O Lord, I simply offer myself to you today as you have commanded. I will serve you forever in humility. Receive me now.

Take, first of all, my sins and consume them with the fire of your love.

And then I turn over to you all that is good in me (though it be insignificant and flawed) that you may add to it and make it acceptable.

I also offer my parents, friends, brothers, sisters—all who are dear to me—and those who have been good to me and to those I love. I bring also those who have asked me to pray for them and for all they love. Protect them from danger; ease their pain; rescue them from evil so they may joyfully thank you.

And I offer prayer especially for those who have hurt me in any way and those I have grieved, innocently or intentionally. Forgive us all equally for our sins and for our offenses against each other. Take away, O Lord, all suspicion, indignation, anger, and contention and anything else that might hinder the love we need for each other.

Have mercy on those who seek your mercy; give grace to those who need it; and make us worthy to come at last to eternal life. Amen.

The Beloved Speaks:

Clearly understand that nothing you can do will make you thoroughly prepared for Communion with me—not even if you should spend an entire year getting ready, and think of nothing else.

It is because of my good generosity that you are invited to come to my table. It is as though a beggar were asked to join a rich man's banquet and all he could offer in return were humble thanks.

Do what you must, and do it well, not out of duty or habit, but with respect, reverence, and affection. I have called you. I have commanded that this be done. I will give you whatever you lack. Come, receive me.

When I make you glow with devotion, thank me. You are not entitled to it, but I have mercy on you.

And if taking this sacrament bores you, keep praying. Sigh and cry for mercy, and keep on doing so until you have at least received some crumb from my table, some drop from my chalice. You need me in a different way than I need you. You do not come to make me holier, but I come to make you better than you were before.

And it is not enough just to prepare for Communion; let the blessing continue when you have left the table. Guard yourself. Let the small talk go. Find some secret place and enjoy me. All the world cannot take me away from you now. I am the one to whom you must give your whole self. From now on, you must live not for yourself, but only for me.

The Follower Speaks:
Lord God, when shall I be united completely with you, and become lost in you, and forget myself absolutely? I want this devotion more than anything else. I am praying and longing to be numbered with the truly devout.

The Beloved Speaks:
When you feel only a little inner devotion, do not fret. Often, only a small thing stands in the way—if you can call anything "small" that interferes with such tremendous good. If you can just remove whatever it is, and overcome it, you will have your desire fulfilled. I place my blessing where I find the container empty.

The Follower Speaks:
Loving Lord, with all devotion I desire you now. You are fully aware of my weakness, my troubled life, my depression. I come to you for healing, tranquility, and confidence. You know all there is to know about me, even my secret thoughts, and you

alone can help me. You know what I need and how great is my emptiness. I stand naked before you.

Refresh your begging servant with spiritual food. Be present with me, illuminating my dark soul. Cut me loose from earthly things and lift up my heart to heavenly things. Don't send me out to wander on my own. You alone are my food and drink, my love and my joy.

With profound devotion and burning love I want to become one with you, O Lord. I hold nothing in reserve, but freely and cheerfully sacrifice myself and everything that is mine to you.

O Lord, my God, you created me and saved me. I desire now with affection, reverence, and gratitude to answer as humbly and devoutly as Mary, the mother of Jesus, "I am the Lord's servant; may it happen to me as you have said" (Luke 1:38).

The Beloved Speaks:
Beware of digging too deeply into the mystery of the sacrament and all matters that are beyond your reach. This has caused many to lose their devotion. You need faith and sincerity, not deep understanding of my great mysteries. If you can't comprehend what is within you, how will you grasp what is beyond you? Submit yourself to me and insights will be added to you in whatever measure you require.

Some have difficulty with the Lord's Supper. This is an indication that the Enemy is at work. Do not trouble yourself too much about it. And do not even try to answer Satan's subtle questions. Trust my Word, and take comfort that unbelievers are not tempted the way the faithful and devout are tempted.

I do not deceive you. I walk with the simple, reveal myself to the humble, give understanding to the poor in spirit, and pour wisdom into pure minds, but I hide from the proudly inquisitive. Human reason is weak and easily led astray, but faith cannot be deceived.

For this reason all scholarship should follow faith, not guide it or intrude upon it. I am, after all, beyond human comprehension and I do things you cannot understand.

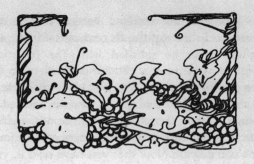

Afterword

While this reinterpretation has resulted in a considerably shortened version of *The Imitation of Christ*, no essential idea has been omitted·from the text. What is missing is the grand style of the original, with the cumulative impact of layer upon layer of repetitive statements relentlessly driving home its central theme of humility. But the gains of this new approach seem to me to offset the losses.

You might want to read one of the complete English versions of this famous book. John Wesley, who produced an abridged version for English Protestants in the eighteenth century, said, "A person will never be satisfied with *The Imitation*, though it were read a thousand times over; for those general principles are the seeds of meditation, and the stores they contain are never exhausted."

Much mystery shrouds the origin of this masterpiece. The earliest extant manuscripts carry no author's name at all. Now that you have read it, you will agree that such an omission is perfectly fitting. The last thing on earth the original writer cared about was seeing his name on a title page. However, a manuscript copy dated 1447, about twenty years after the original was completed, does bear the name of Thomas à Kempis, and most copies from then on repeat the claim.

Still, more than two dozen others have been suggested as the actual author, with Thomas à Kempis being reduced to editor. Of the arguments put forward, only two candidates seem worthy of consideration: Jean de Gerson, Chancellor of the University of Paris, and Gerhard Groote, founder of the religious community Thomas à Kempis joined.

Jean de Gerson, who died in 1429, is listed as author on some very early editions of *The Imitation*. A manuscript dated 1460 makes such a claim and a few printed copies from later years also attribute the work to him. The reasons for rejecting Gerson as the actual author are quite convincing. He was a priest; not a monk. The style, quotations, and themes in this little book are less likely those of a University Chancellor, and more likely those of a member of the Brotherhood of the Common Life, about which more will be said below.

Gerhard Groote, on the other hand, is a serious competitor who is widely accepted as author because of scholarly research in our own time. James von Ginnekin and Joseph Malaise have shown interesting parallels between *The Imitation of Christ* and the *Spiritual Diary of Gerhard Groote*. Groote's troubled life could well have been the source of many hard lessons taught with such conviction. A successful canon lawyer in Deventer, Holland, he suffered a serious illness which helped him recognize the emptiness of his prosperous life. In 1374 Groote gave up most of his fortune, surrendered his lucrative positions, and dedicated his life to spiritual discipline. For three years he lived according to the strict asceticism of the Carthusian monastery. After this time of training and testing, he returned to the outside, preaching to people of their need for deeper devotion to God. From 1379 to 1383 the Netherlands responded favorably to his call to discipleship. But Groote criticized the leadership of the church in the process, and ecclesiastical machinery turned against him. The bishop took away his license and ordered him to stop preaching. Crushed, Groote returned home and lived in obscurity. Others who had responded to his message joined him there and began organizing The Brotherhood of the Common Life, whose members followed a way of life they called *Devotio Moderna*. The Brotherhood grew to become the leading educators of Northern Europe's children just prior to the Renaissance.

Arguing against Groote's authorship is the fact that not one of the seven hundred surviving early manuscripts bears his name. Moreover, none of the Brotherhood's members ever claimed that *The Imitation of Christ* was written by their founder.

After examining the arguments for and against these and many other possible authors, we come once again to Thomas Haemerken (variously spelled Hamerken, Haemerlein) of Kempen, Germany. It is Thomas whose name actually appears on so many early manuscripts. Two typical inscriptions read: "This book was made by Thomas à Kempis, regular at Mount St. Agnes near Zwolle," and, "Finished and completed in the year of our Lord 1441 by the hand of brother Thomas von Kempen at Mount St. Agnes near Zwolle." Whether his name was put there as author, editor, or copyist is an issue that will be debated forever.

Thomas of Kempen was sent as a child to Deventer to live and study with the Brothers of the Common Life. He was later ordained a priest in the Roman Catholic church in 1413 and entered a monastery begun by the Brothers at Zwolle. Those were the uncertain days before the Protestant Reformation, and the politics of church and state pressed heavily upon Thomas and his contemporaries. The death of his older brother, of whom he was exceptionally fond, was indirectly caused by the upheaval of the times. If the content of *The Imitation of Christ* requires an author of great sensitivity who had been rocked by overwhelming circumstances, but found peace through God's "inner consolation," Thomas certainly qualifies.

The work is most often published under his name because he qualifies on nearly every point. The discovery of provocative similarities in the writings of others justifies responsible caution in naming Thomas à Kempis as the sole author, but there can be little doubt that he had a major, probably the primary, role in its production.

Thomas à Kempis died in 1471 at age 92, thirty years after finishing the work. He finally found the resting place of perfect devotion that was his life's goal. Marking his grave in Zwolle, Holland, are these words:

> *"Honori, non memoriae,*
> *THOMAE KEMPENSIS,*
> *cujus nomen perennius*
> *quam monumentum"*

> "To the honor, not the memory,
> OF THOMAS À KEMPIS,
> whose name will endure longer
> than a monument."

ORDERING
YOUR
PRIVATE WORLD

with Study Guide

by

GORDON MacDONALD

Awarded the Gold Medallion for the Best Devotional
Book of the Year.

'*One of the most helpful books I've read in twenty years.*'
Gavin Reid

'*I wish that I had read it years ago.*'

Billy Graham

A new edition to help you obtain the maximum benefit
from a life-changing message.

HIGHLAND BOOKS

RESTORING YOUR SPIRITUAL PASSION

by

GORDON MacDONALD

We are working harder, playing longer, buying more and yet we are enjoying life less. Why is there so much dissatisfaction with our lives? *Restoring Your Spiritual Passion* gives the reasons and answers to our dilemma.

Here are practical steps to help you escape the pervasive sense of spiritual tiredness that has settled into your life. They will re-open the 'rivers of living water' and help quench your inner thirst.

'*All who mean business with God could find their batteries recharged by getting to grips with this book.*'
Christian Arena

HIGHLAND BOOKS